Endorsements

Denise Shick's edited book, Understanding Gender Confusion, provides some helpful material from a conservative Christian perspective on the thorny subject of transgenderism. Denise can speak from two helpful vantage points: as someone whose life as a child was impacted negatively by a father who viewed himself as a woman; and as someone who now ministers on a regular basis to families dealing with transgender concerns. The book also includes interesting testimonies from persons who have struggled with desires to be a different sex than they were born to be. We live in a world that values stories. The particular strength of this work is that it offers a number of stories that may cause readers to rethink parts of the prevailing media-driven narrative on transgenderism.

Robert A. J. Gagnon, Ph.D. Associate Professor of New Testament Pittsburgh Theological Seminary Author of: The Bible and Homosexual Practice (Abingdon Press)

Denise Shick is uniquely qualified to discuss gender confusion. She addresses the topic with the experience of a family members struggle as well as the support of others who speak, write and live with daily freedom from confusion. But, perhaps most significantly, Denise approaches this sensitive topic with the compassion and grace of God that brings healing not condemnation. Denise is that rare gem of a person whose deep faith in God has given her the strength to address a delicate subject with a heart to heal.

Rev. Brad Preston
Sawyer Evangelical Church
Eastern Conference,
Evangelical Church Superintendent

Gender Confusion Understanding offers readers excellent testimonies and case examples of persons who have struggled with gender confusion, including gender identity disorder (GID). First and third person accounts document how the causes and consequences of this condition and the persons' responses to it have affected themselves and their families. Particularly moving are stories of persons who regret having used hormone therapy and plastic surgery to try to live as transgender or trans, i.e. to more closely resemble and try to act as if they were a person of the opposite sex. ng with offering examples from her own personal life and from many years of ministry, the author, Denise Shick, provides an overview of the major influences in our modern culture which engender the development of gender identity disorder and which influence persons to try to appear and live as the opposite sex. She discusses personal and scientific descriptions of the self-harming and ultimately self-defeating consequences of trendy medical responses, including "sexual reassignment" surgery. *Understanding Gender Confusion* offers practicing Christians hopeful encouragement, challenging exhortation, and wise advice about understanding gender identity and responding to it helpfully in light of the truth and with the resources of their faith.

Philip M. Sutton, Ph.D.
Licensed Psychologist and Marriage and Family Therapist

The world has become a confusing place and this is not because moral truth is ambiguous. We now live in a culture where the tail is wagging the dog, where commonsense is replaced by fidelity to the visceral. Biological and spiritual truth has been supplanted by the loudest and most vehement voices. Fortunately, where dysfunction, confusion, rejection, and sexual assault have occurred, God's grace, redemption, healing, and transformation are available for those who reach out for them. Denise Shick understands this subject as few people do. For those who are confused by the full scale assault and widespread propaganda forced on us daily, Shick clarifies the issues as few have done. This should be mandatory reading by every leader, student, and anyone interested in the truth about gender confusion.

Don S. Otis
Author, Whisker Rubs: Developing the Masculine Identity Founder of Veritas Communications

Understanding Gender Confusion

A Faith-based Perspective

Denise Shick
Editor

Acknowledgements

I wish to thank my mentor who took me under his wing to teach me all that he could. I'd also like to thank the Board of Directors of *Help4Families* who believes in the ministry God has called us to.

Dedication

I wish to thank my dear mother, Ruth Sophia who instilled the value and importance of persevering through life's difficult circumstances.

About

Denise Shick and *Help4Families*

Denise Shick is the founder and Executive Director of *Help 4 Families*. *Help 4 Families* is a non-profit Christian ministry dedicated to offer encouragement and resources for those who struggle with gender confusion and their friends, families, and communities.

Denise has worked with families of gender confusion since 2004.

She diligently works along side of church leaders in order to bring an understanding of the emotional and spiritual confusion when a loved one has gender confusion. She has led church-based support groups for people with sexual addictions.

She is the author of *My Daddy's Secret* and *When Hope Seems Lost* and co-author of "Dangerous Affirmations." She is a national speaker and has been interviewed on several Christian radio and Christian television programs.

Denise and her husband Mark have been married for 33 years.

CONTENTS

Introduction

This book offers several first-hand testimonies from individuals who have struggled with gender confusion, yet found understanding and freedom. Is freedom from gender confusion truly possible? This book will help you understand, from a faith-based perspective, how and why. This book also offers educational pieces to help you understand the dynamics of gender confusion, societal shifts, and the dangers associated with hormonal and surgical interventions.

The chapter, "Escaping Femininity" I will discuss some of the dynamics necessary to understand female gender confusion and on the same token, the chapter "Fleeing Masculinity" I will discuss, through case illustration, some dynamics necessary to understand male gender confusion, based on a Christian perspective.

Understanding and responding to families affected by gender confusion is also important, therefore the chapter on "Family Difficulties" will help in this process. One person's gender confusion can cause multiple issues for the family members. Most families feel as if they are abandoned and alone. They can't see what's coming their way or what's behind them. They try to grab hold of the situation only to find that it's like grabbing a fist full of fog. Affected family members often feel as if they are in desert, spiritually starved and parched.

They have a longing for God's living water and hunger for His love and embrace. What is needed is a Christian community response. Those that are hurting are seeking a Christ-like church, not a culture-accepting church.

In the chapter, "Cross-dressing and Christianity," the author discusses how he was raised in a feminized environment, and learned that the role of a woman was "dominant," something he had always longed for in his life. The idea of cross-dressing was his way to neutralize his feelings of inadequacy as a man. Cross-dressing had become adaptive and was his "…secret world where [he] would fantasize about being beautiful and soft." But, deep inside he knew this was not God's intent for him, and that God had made him a man who was indeed wonderfully made, and adequate just as he was. Finally, after 30 years of dealing with cross-dressing he reveals the freedom he found.

In the chapter, "What do you Really Want," Kerry reveals an understanding of his troubled past. Kerry's mother instilled a "…profound disappointment that he has not been born a girl." Consequently, he would shun his own masculinity. He felt he was "a failure" for not being the girl his mother always wanted. Leaning to that which seemed palliative at the time, Kerry would dress in mother's clothes. In this chapter Kerry reveals his journey, one that is spiritual, and one that ends in his understanding of God's grace. Kerry says profoundly, "By God's grace I am becoming the integrated human being the Lord designed me to."

In the chapter, "A Journey of Healing," the author discusses how she wanted to be a boy instead of a girl, and how she vowed one day she would undergo sex reassignment surgery. However, her journey took a different path and she now testifies, "…I am finally coming out of the closet in a redemptive way, sharing my story with others to bring hope and restoration."

In the chapter, "Beauty To Ashes" the author reveals her heart's "desire to know God the Father on a deep, meaningful level and allowing room for God to heal areas in my life is where my true healing began   .

In conjunction with faith-based testimonies, this book is educational in purpose. Despite the current societal trends to give hormones to children and adults with gender identity disorders or gender identity disphoria, the chapter on "Dangers of Hormone Therapy" will reveal the array of problems hormonal therapies contribute; it appears hormonal interventions are simply not a safe course for individuals, and especially children, to take.

Sex reassignment surgery, like hormonal therapy does not change the fact that one is genetically male or female. Often times those who have undergone these surgeries have regrets. In the chapter "Sex Reassignment Surgery Regrets" you will read and understand the real life painful regrets that these surgeries can bring.

The chapter on "The Shifting of Society" discusses how science and educational systems how been ransacked with political correctness and simply ignore the dangers of gender confusion and the possibility of change. Despite our culture's shift, it is imperative for people of faith to resist caving in to the culture's co change to counter the prevailing messages out there today.

The chapter on "Steps to Freedom" is vital in that it provides an honest look at what's necessary to find freedom.

1

The Shifting of Society: A Slippery Slope

James E. Phelan

From a "mad scientist" to the "Sexual Revolution"

With so-called academic "scientists" such as Dr. Alfred Kinsey paving a false legacy that sexual deviations were commonplace, it is no wonder the hedonistic *Sexual Revolution* evolved creating the perception that "anything goes," tearing down American values of chastity and fidelity. In the 1970's *homosexuality*, for example, was no longer seen as abnormal because Dr. Kinsey and some followers said that it was common

(Reisman, 2010). This opened the door for other academics to disregard pretty much anything else as sexually abnormal (Moser & Kleinplate, 2006).

Paraphilias, once deviation, now politically correct

Today transgenderism, once seen as an abnormal psychiatric condition (paraphilia) is now considered in many circles as "normal," and in fact, in many outlets, even encouraged. Some academics feel paraphilias in general do not meet standards for a mental health disorder classification (Moser & Kleinplate, 2006). When large influential health and mental health organizations, seen as authoritative, dictate what is considered normal and appropriate, it is no wonder society and legislations follows suit. This is the case with major organizations especially in the U.S. who strongly suggest transgenderism be accepted as a normal way of life and all efforts advocated towards full acceptance (American Psychological Association, 2009; American Medical Association, 2011; American Psychiatric Association, 2012).

Never before has transgenderism been so politicalized. No U.S. President in history has been verbally affirmative for sexual minority rights until Barack Obama. Recently, President Obama and former U. S. Secretary of State, Hillary Clinton called for equal rights for transgenderism and now advocate for full global acceptance (Labott, 2011). Protections for transsexuals continue to multiply as litigations expand "sex discrimination," in general to cover various types of discriminations against transgendered people (Juarez & Williams, 2013; Phoenix, n.d).

The evolving education system

Gender conformity was once a sacred part of the educational and societal process. Boys socialized and role modeled with other boys, and girls with girls. Gender roles were seen as binary having unique and differing characteristics, yet complementary to each other. As society evolved towards a liberal path, down a slippery slope, the roles and clarity of gender and sexuality became blurred and abstract.

Not only do many educators demand acceptance and tolerance for lesbians, gays, bisexuals, and transgenders (LGBT) some enforce values that otherwise would be prohibitive of students, especially faith-oriented students. Many students and parents feel that "student diversity training", or national themed programs such as "Day of Silence", or "Diversity Days", which includes teaching that the LGBT lifestyle is appropriate, is rather a Trojan Horse promoting broader agendas. Public education advocates like to point out, for example, that parents have no constitutional right to have their child opt out of mandatory "student diversity training" (National Education Association, 2006). But, in California public schools students can use any restroom or locker rooms of the gender they "identify with" beginning in Kindergarten! In one high school in California, students even elected a transgender teen as their homecoming queen (MacBride, 2013).

The faith and religious values of students was once highly respected in the educational system, however now if students express disapproval of LGBT agendas or curriculums, based on their religion convictions, their beliefs are often opinioned as archaic, intolerable, unwelcomed, wrong, and even hateful. The NEA does say however, that "In 'open forum' type events (including those initiated by students or outside groups), schools probably would be well advised to accommodate viewpoints against [LGBT] as long as they are not lewd, vulgar, indecent, clearly offensive, or would substantially interfere with school operations or the rights of others" (National Education

Association, 2006, p. 17). However, when the non-profit organization Parents and Friends of Ex-Gays & Gays (PFOX) sent the NEA material to include in their comprehensive outreach efforts to support an inclusive environment for the ex-gay community, an NEA staff member wrote back to them saying, *"Please stop sending us you're* [sic] *garbage. Sincerely, the Majority of America"* (PFOX, n.d.).

Television: No longer a safe place

Families once watched television together without much fear of being exposed to an immensity of immoral images and messages. Those days are long gone. Now prime time and even daytime television airing shows like *Dancing with the Stars* (Chaz Bono episodes), *Glee*, *Modern Family*, and *Ellen* glamorize transgenderism, homosexuality, and other deviated lifestyles exposing vulnerable children to confusing messages. However, not all mental health experts feel this is right:

> The last thing vulnerable children and adolescents need, as they wrestle with the normal process of establishing their identities, is to watch a captive crowd in a studio audience applaud on cue for someone whose search for an identity culminated with the removal of her breasts, the injection of steroids and, perhaps one day soon, the

fashioning of a make-shift phallus to replace her vagina (Quoted by Dr. Dr. Keith Ablow, 2011).

However, those who agree with experts such as Dr. Ablow, or attempt to steer their children from acceptance of the LGBT lifestyle are often labeled as "homophobic," "transphobic," or "heterosexist".

Religious shifts

While the majority mainstream religions such as Catholics, Hindus, Jews, Muslims, and Protestants hold on strong to the view that the abandonment of one's born and God-given gender is a sin, some secondary religious circles are shifting (e.g. as in the cases of some sects of Episcopalian, Methodist and the United Church of Christ). Some have shifted towards radical extremes to where major emphases of the church are on LGBT acceptance and celebrations. In many of these churches clergy are often LGBT themselves (e.g. as in the cases of the Unitarian Universalist Association and the Metropolitan Community Churches). The Metropolitan Community Churches (MCC) strongly embeds themselves in politics for causes such as marriage equality advocacy (Kane, 2013). The Metropolitan Community Churches actually has specific ministries for the transgendered and sets out to train other church congregations to offer tools and resources to create, enhance, and maintain gender non-conforming-focused "ministries" (Kane, 2013).

Other shifts have occurred as well. Organizations such as SoulForce now exist, and label themselves as non-profit and faith-based, set out to police mainstream churches' college campus telling them how wrong they are about their views that homosexuality is a sin and that the abandonment of one's born and God-given gender is a sin. They aggressively, yet peacefully implement dialogues and demonstrations on campuses and other venues set out to shame Christian students and personnel suggesting their ways are demeaning and hurtful to the LGBT community. Groups like these emerge with radical binary ideas that sexual minority statuses are bestowed blessings rather than a human struggle, that a person's sexual preference is innate, not a choice (Chavez, 2004).

Despite our culture's shift, it is imperative for people of faith to resist caving in to the culture's confused gender messages. Persons of faith are in a fight like none other before and need to persevere, as Paul did. Despite being imprisoned, Paul continued to reach other inmates with the truth of God's Word. Many today are trying to silence people of faith and their belief that transgenderism is not God's natural intent.

2

The Politics Of Gender Identity Disorder

James E. Phelan

Politics and the Diagnostic and Statistical Manual of Mental Disorders

The newest edition of the American Psychiatric Association's

(APA) *Diagnostic and Statistical Manual of Mental Disorders*, or

DSM-5, replaced the diagnostic term "Gender Identity Disorder"

(GID) with the term "Gender Dysphoria," but GID is still used in

various circles. While advocates wanted to normalize the

condition of gender nonconformity, and felt that mental diagnosis

was stigmatizing, they still wanted a formal diagnosis instituted so individuals could have access to cross-sex hormones, gender reassignment surgery, and social and legal transition (e.g. defense for transgender people who have experienced discrimination based on their gender identity).

Advocates criticized psychiatry for pathologizing transgenderism and so they pressured the APA to change the language. The APA admits that its change was to be sensitive to special interests groups, rather than as a result of overwhelming empirical and field data to support changing the diagnosis of GID. This pattern was generally the case for many areas of the DSM-5 (Allen, 2010). Homosexuality was voted out of a previous edition of the DSM in the 1970's due to social pressure from gay activists, rather than for scientific justification (Bayer, 1987).

The APA now assets that gender nonconformity is not in itself a mental disorder. However, the critical element of gender dysphoria is the presence of clinically significant distress associated with the condition. The focus on "distress" now however is generally on the distress over the gender (now seen as the condition), not the gender disorder itself (historically seen as the condition).

Advocates of the change argue that the former diagnosis of GID just stigmatized people and actually backfired on their social agenda needs. The DSM is about social culture satisfaction integrating criteria enough so that it is billable and at the same time meeting social demands. Many organizations are now saying that transgenderism should be perceived in a medical model rather than a psychological model. They argue that many anatomical inconsistencies now can be corrected surgically or chemically to align with the experienced true self. This is contrary to previous practice whereas the attempts to intervene with children suffering from GID were to help them ameliorate the condition from a psychological and behavioral perspective (Zucker & Bradley, 1995).

Politics and the court system

With achievements in normalization of gender disorders transgendered individuals and advocates are now using the legal, court and political system to achieve special rights. The media is filled with these types of transactions. For example, Massachusetts' Department of Elementary and Secondary Education informed grade school principals that they must allow boys and girls of any age who self-identify as transgender to play on sports teams designated for their preferred genders, and use the public school bathroom and locker room of their choosing (Andersen, 2013). This was done even if the student has not had reconstructive surgery and despite other student's discomfort. So, young ladies are now forced to be in the bathroom and locker room with biological males. In Maine, a school that refuses to follow similar guidelines were found to be in violation of the state's antidiscrimination law (Sharp, 2014).

Caution

The American College of Pediatricians cautions educators and others about the management of students exhibiting symptoms of gender confusion. These concerns are outlined in a letter and fact sheet sent by College president Thomas Benton, MD, to all the nation's school district superintendents. Dr. Benton also alerts them to a new Web resource, FactsAboutYouth.com, which was created by a coalition of health professionals to provide factual information to educators, parents, and students about sexual development. "As pediatricians, our primary interest is in the health and well-being of children and youth," Dr. Den Trumbull,

Vice President of the College explains. "We are increasingly concerned that in too many instances, misinformation or incorrect assumptions are guiding well-intentioned educators to adopt policies that are actually harmful to those youth dealing with sexual confusion."

The College reminds school superintendents that it is not uncommon for adolescents to experience transient confusion about their gender or sexual orientation and that most students will ultimately adopt a heterosexual orientation if not otherwise encouraged. For this reason, schools should not seek to develop policy which "affirms" or encourages these non-heterosexual attractions among students who may merely be experimenting or experiencing temporary sexual confusion. Such premature labeling can lead some adolescents to engage in behaviors that carry serious physical and mental health risks.

The College asserts that there is no scientific evidence that anyone is born gay or transgendered. Therefore, the College advises that schools should not teach or imply to students that homosexual attraction is innate, always life-long and unchangeable. Literature does show that efforts to restore heterosexual attraction can be effective for some people (Phelan, 2014).

Finally, The College states that optimal health and respect for all students can only be achieved within a school by first respecting the rights of students and parents to accurate information and to self-determination. It is the school's legitimate role to provide a safe environment for respectful self-expression for all students. It is not the school's role to diagnose or attempt to treat any student's medical condition, and certainly not the school's role to engage and mingle in the business of students' perceived sexual orientation.

3

Dangers of Hormone Treatments

James E. Phelan

Many transgendered people will seek out ways to transition from their birth gender to the opposite gender. Whether or not transgendered persons actually pursue sex reassignment surgery, it is not uncommon for some individuals to engage in hormone therapies. With more acceptance of GID and educational and mental health organizations promoting that these individuals pursue transgender lifestyles, children prescribed hormones to block their gender specific puberty (GnRH analogs), and those to increase opposite sex characteristic (estrogen or testosterone) are on the rise. Some medical providers make the sympathetic case that since GID children are at high risk for suicide, running away, and using "black market" hormones, medically supervised treatment should be made available.

The use of GnRH analogs will suppress menses in girls due to lack of estrogen and in boys will block the development of fertility due to lack of testosterone. This is an extreme form of biology intervention for children whose brains are not fully developed. While decision-making centers in the child's mind are not matured, parents fulfilling desired opposite-sex want-a-be childhood fantasies through invasive hormonal intervention equates maniacal.

And what are the potential consequences of hormonal intervention? Actually they are multifaceted and complicated. To interfere with the natural biological direction of one's body and chemistry cannot go without consequence. Girls who are prescribed GnRHa are at a great risk for bone growth delay, which then will require the administration of growth stimulating drugs to help assist in achieving an acceptable male height (Delemarre-van de Waal & Cohen-Kettenis, 2006). However, growth-stimulating drugs also have consequential side effects. For those who begin cross hormones as adolescents, exposure to hormone-dependent tumors is greatly increased over the course of a lifetime (Gooren, Giltay, & Bunck, 2008).

Studies of male-to-female (m-to-f) transsexuals on estrogen and GnRHa treatment revealed a statistically significant increase in weight, total body fat, and visceral fat, decrease in insulin sensitivity, and in some cases increases in blood pressure. Female-to-male (f-to-m) transsexuals on testosterone and GnRHa treatment also resulted in a statistically significant increase in body weight and body mass index (BMI).

Other statistically significant changes that negatively affect cardiovascular health in f-to-m transsexuals are increased HDL cholesterol, triglycerides, and decreased insulin sensitivity (Gooren, et al, 2008). In men, abnormally low levels of testosterone are associated with insulin resistance, which eventually can result in Type II diabetes. In one study, the occurrence of venous thromboembolism (blood clots) increased 20-fold in m-to-f patients treated with estrogens and antiandrogens (Van Kesteren, et al, 1997).

Cardiovascular disease is also a concern. Oral estrogen therapy has been shown to increase levels of the inflammatory and hemostatic markers interleukin-6, C-reactive protein, and factor IX, all of which may be predictive of future cardiovascular disease (Knezevich, et al, 2012).

Cancer and cancer risk is associated with hormonal therapies. Cases of breast carcinoma in m-to-f patients on estrogen treatment have been reported, as have breast fibroadenomas. Breast cancer has also been reported in a f-to-m transsexual post-bilateral mastectomy while on testosterone treatment. The ovaries of f-to-m transsexuals receiving testosterone treatment look similar to polycystic ovaries, which are more likely to develop malignancies (Gooren, 1999; Gooren et al., 2008). A high prevalence of endometrial hyperplasia has been noted in a study of transgender men undergoing hysterectomy (Futterweit, & Deligdisch, 1986).

Hormones are common mood interferes. For example, research shows that some transgender individuals report mood swings, increased anger, and increased aggressiveness after starting androgen therapy (Israel & Tarver, 1997).

As stated earlier, to interfere with the natural biological direction of one's body and chemistry does not go without consequence. With research indicating hormonal therapies contributing to bone problems, lipid disorders, mood disorders, cardiovascular disease, malignancies, and other pathologies, it appears hormonal interventions are not a safe course for individuals, especially children, to take.

4

Fleeing Masculinity

Denise Shick

I was waiting to board a flight when I noticed two young men that appeared to be a couple. One of the men appeared to be approximately 18 to 20 years old. He had a dark complication, black hair, and brown eyes. But perhaps most noticeable about him was the strong feminine body language he displayed. He gracefully moved his hand toward his boyfriend's face in the exact manner that a woman would slide her hand gently over her male partner's face. Next I heard his voice. As he giggled and spoke, his tone reminded me of a 12-year-old girl.

His partner was a handsome 25-year-old man. His appearance was such that a mother might pick him out of a crowd as potential husband material for her daughter. He was tall, with blue eyes, blonde hair, and a neatly trimmed beard and mustache. He placed his hand over his partner's shoulder as they smiled at each other. When I located my seat on the plane, I discovered that the masculine partner would be sitting next to me during the flight. We had a pleasant conversation as he shared his love for the children he instructs as a music teacher in an elementary school.

Later in the conversation he spoke of the time he spent with his family. Then he said that "we"—that is, he and his male "fiancée"—had gone home so that his family could meet him. He spoke of their relationship with no hint of secrecy. And why not? Society has widely accepted same-sex relationships, "gay marriage", and gender reversal surgeries as perfectly "normal".

The Effect on Families and Society

Sadly, young men are fleeing from masculinity instead of embracing their true identity. Our society no longer embraces or encourages traditional gender roles. Many men are aimlessly trying to discover, on their own, what it actually means to be a man. Many men are not confident in knowing how to embrace their masculinity because they have been wounded emotionally and/or sexually and, as a result, have deep scars of rejections. This gender confusion is devastating to families and to society.

What is the negative impact on families? Let's start with an honest look at children raised by two dads. If the child is a girl, she has no mother figure to teach her how to embrace and discover her femininity. The mother teaches through her own actions how to nurture and walk in the woman's role. A mother plays a crucial role in her son's development as well. A son learns how to treat a girl from both of his parents. What's more, he learns gender roles as he observes how his mother nurtures those in her care. As a son grows, a wise mother gradually releases him from her sphere and into his father's sphere of influence, which develops his masculinity (Gresh, 2012).

A child who has two "dads" or two "moms" has no opportunity to see firsthand God's perfect creation of the family unit. Our culture has fallen to the devil's trap that blurs and confuses gender differences and roles. A boy needs a balance of love and attention from a mother, who is secure in her femininity, and father who is secure in his masculinity, who both love and care for each other. Boys especially need a godly father to role model the principles he needs to mature in his own masculinity (Dobson, 2001).

The Power of Repeated Lies

I have often heard men confess that they have thoughts that something was wrong with them, that they should have been born female. If they hear the thoughts and whispers often enough, they begin to believe them, especially when the lies have haunted them since their childhood. Consider this: When an adult male says he remembered "feeling this way"—that he was supposed to have been born female—since he was young, he might be telling the truth. He might not remember a time when he did not feel "this way." That doesn't mean, however, he was born that way. It likely means that he's heard the thoughts and suggestions for as long as he can remember.

Joseph Goebbels, said, "If you tell a lie big enough and keep repeating it, people will eventually come to believe it." If a male repeatedly hears the lie that he was meant to be a woman, eventually he will believe it—and be likely to act on it. The same is true of a female who repeatedly hears—in her thoughts or from others—that she was meant to be a man.

Some men are running from feelings of depression, relational problems, drug or alcohol addictions, suicidal tendencies, and other psychotic issues. These men are abandoning their masculinity and their traditional role because they are weary from battling their thought life and society's celebration of non-traditional attitudes and behaviors. Some really don't understand why they struggle with thoughts that encourage them to make decisions that dramatically alter their lives.

Leonard's impulses to cross dress and fantasies of becoming a woman have become problematic for him. Leonard wants to understand the root issue for his behavior. In addition to seeing a therapist, he also has a support system. No matter how fearful reality may be; he will finally come to an understand his behavior and mindset. Leonard believes that discovering the factors which underlies his condition is necessary in order to help him move forward.

LGBT organizations have convinced many politicians that gender transformations are necessary because people who yearn for gender changes believe that they were "born that way," (albeit an unproven theory). To deny them access to procedures that fulfill their inborn desires is cruel and unjust, they say.

Politicians and professionals actually need to examine for themselves the causes of such desires. Then, when they discover the truth, they can encourage and support programs that treat these confused people and help them to work toward the healing process. Sex-reassignment surgery changes only the outside, the "shell." The person's genetic structure remains the same as it was before the surgery and hormone treatments. Inside, a male person remains a male person, likewise a female remains a female.

The Reasons for Capitulation

Despite our culture's glamorization of men who "embrace their true feminine identity," there is no real proof that some men were really meant to be women.

It's more likely that men who have these struggles have them because others have told them, perhaps repeatedly, that they should have been a girl. Or, they're men who felt rejected by one or both of their parents, or, when they were children, older children or adults molested them, so they began to fantasize about being a woman in order to escape reality. It's complex and many circumstances can contribute to being confused about one's gender.

So why is it more common to help these confused people obtain a gender change than to really search for and treat the underlying causes? It's likely that the first reason for this capitulation is political. The LGBT lobby is powerful, extremely militant and vocal. Giving in to their demands is easier than resisting them.

The second reason is financial. As the saying goes, "Money makes the world go round." Sex reassignment surgery for a male can cost between $15,000 and $35,000 or more, plus much follow-up and ongoing care. Multiply that number by thousands of confused young people and that's a lot of money generated for the medical and pharmaceutical professions. Then, after spending all that money, and after the patient's body has been modified to match how he felt, at some point in his life, the "feeling" might change. Typically those who desire SRS experience high anxiety and excessive level of depression.

How much wiser would it have been for the professionals to have rooted out and treated the underlying emotional and other causes of the patient's desires? Wiser, perhaps, but probably not as lucrative for the medical professionals who have treated him.

Jason felt rejection by his father for most of his life. He suffered physical, sexual and verbal abuse as a child. By the age of 17 he left home, and he had some contact with his mother during his "street" time. According to Jason, he had over 200 male lovers. While living as a transgendered "woman" he had two failed marriages. As we discussed his life and choices, he admitted, "I get such a thrill when I walk by and become noticed by men. I watch their heads turn towards me as they whistle at me." He's had several surgical procedures that have created an illusory of an identity that he continues to struggle. Jason claims he does not know who he wants to be.

Regrets When It's Too Late

The *International Journal of Transgenderism* has published evidence that many patients regret their sex-reassignment surgery when they discover that the surgery failed to solve their real problems. Some subjects confessed that they had second thoughts about having the surgery. However, because they feared that they might never get another chance at the surgery, they kept those second thoughts to themselves (Kuiper, & Cohen-Kettenis 1998).

My own father believed that becoming a woman would make his life more satisfying and fulfilling. He, like so many others, then discovered that fulfilling his fantasy did not give him the inner peace he'd sought after that was because his problem was emotional, not physical (Shick, 2008).

A 23-year-old man called me saying he was calling for a friend. It took only seconds to determine that he was really calling for himself. He had the sex-reassignment surgery six months earlier. He felt desperate because he recognized that there was no going back. He asked, "How can my friend forgive himself for what he has done?"

Sexual reassignment surgery is not simple, but highly invasive. According to caring professionals:

> Efforts should be directed toward the development of effective therapy for adolescents and adults. The fact that such therapy is not described extensively in the literature and therefore is not widely available, and that these patients resist therapeutic interventions, does not justify

giving in to the demand for surgical mutilation (Fitzgibbons, Sutton, & O' Leary, 2009, p. 125).

A mom and dad were shocked to learn that their son was living a homosexual lifestyle and was transitioning to a female. They were a close family, and their son had never given them any grief. Before long, their son started to take illegal hormones and became further depressed as he started to transition to a woman. He felt as if he was in between the male and female world, and he had no peace. About a year and a half later he committed suicide, stating he could not live in that confused state of mind any longer.

Parents with sucidal children are often desperate for the medical field to help them. And some men with G.I.D. or gender dysphoria do seek counseling, support, and other tools that will help them learn the causes that have stirred up their confusion. They want to accept and embrace their masculinity rather then flee from it. Such choices are brave and right, but they are not easy. There is no quick fix for such a difficult issue.

Meet Luke, who suffers from severe anxiety, depression, and compulsive behaviors. Luke is confused about his male identity and feels inadequate as a man. His cross-dressing become unmanageable. He quietly admits that he feels 'good' when cross-dressing, but hates himself afterwards. Luke has grown tired and worn from the bondage of his addictive behaviors. He is now seeing a therapist on a regular basis. Some visits with his therapist are challenging due to the "stuff" that he has to face. As tough as it is sometimes, he is experiencing some freedom as he comes to understand his root issues. He is determined to move forward towards being free.

People suffering from gender confusion must want help, just like anyone else with a problem that has become addictive. They need to know that recovery will not be easy, but they also need to be encouraged that by discovering the underlying factors in their life. The darkness can be lifted. Most gender-confused men don't know why they feel feminine, so they accept the propaganda that tells them they were "born that way". Then, pride often stops them from seeking the healing they really need. A person in such a situation needs encouragement and a strong and godly support system to help get them through it.

If I could say just one thing to each mother with a son, it would be this: Please do not dress him in girl's clothing, and for heaven's sake, never tell him that you'd wished for a girl instead of a boy. Such words can cause the boy to feel rejected, and can become a breaking point that leads him to seek another identity in order to serve and please his mother. Feeling rejected by the father, whether the rejection is real or perceived, can have similarly troubling results. Despite the old saying, words can harm, often far worse than sticks and stones.

Discovering and Dealing With the Root Causes

In dealing with such hurts, one must work through some deep wounds. We can pretend those dealing with GID were simply "born this way" and have no choice in the matter. But denial is not a healthy option—not for the struggler, or for his parent, spouse, child, or friend. Sooner or later that big pink-elephant balloon of denial will explode, leading to further devastation.

Some men, during their childhood, watched their fathers abuse their mothers, which then led them to vow to be different. Sometimes they take that vow too far; they choose to become as different from their father as possible—to become a woman.

Jim remembers, as a young boy, trying to protect his mother from the abuse he saw his father inflict upon his mother and sister—including sexual abuse of his sister. Jim concluded that, "If that's what being a man is about, I want no part of it."

Jake, on the other hand, recalls his father favoring his older sister. Jake believed that if he had been born a girl his father would have displayed the affection that Jake desired.

The next scenario is a bit unlike the other two I have just given. Sometimes I hear from people who say they had a wonderful family life, good parents, and positive nurturing. Even so, they have fallen into an addictive state of cross-dressing and fantasies when a one-time experiment turned into an inescapable whirlpool.

Thomas stated, "No one knows that beneath my pilot's uniform I'm wearing women's underwear." He continued: "I thought I could control it, but I've learned that it now controls me." He feels that each event takes him deeper into an inexorable vortex of deception and lies. I have heard Thomas's words often from those who are naïve about the addiction cycle.

The intense inner conflict these people experience is serious, and often life-altering. Again, remember that most of them truly believe they were born in the wrong body—the wrong gender.

Some have told me, "I tried to castrate myself," or "If I cannot transition, then I want to die." Some, as we have read in this chapter, do in fact commit suicide. Suicide thoughts and surgically removing healthy body parts to match a person's feelings are not normal.

Dr. Paul McHugh, a former Professor of Psychiatry at the Johns Hopkins says, "We have wasted scientific and technical resources and damaged our professional creditability by collaborating with madness rather than trying to study, cure and ultimately prevent it". Dr. McHugh admits that he has witnessed a great deal of damage from regrets of sex-reassignment (McHugh, 2004). "Persons who desire SRS typically experience serious emotional conflicts, often complicated by sexual self-rejection and depression" (Fitzgibbons, Sutton, & O'Leary, 2009, p. 111).

In one instance, a man who admitted to have been sexually abused by his older brother from the age of seven to fourteen desired to have a vagina. He stated, "I will sacrifice everything to change. If you have a vagina you can control people." Although he is afraid of intercourse, he felt that he would be safe physiologically if penetrated through an artificial vagina, as he had been hurt physiologically by anal sex (Fitzgibbons, Sutton, & O'Leary, 2009, p. 115).

A Faith-based Response

The mind is a powerful tool; it can control our thoughts and actions in a negative way that is filled with potentially lethal consequences. Satan knows exactly where and how to slip into a life in which there is a crack in the door to a person's heart and soul. This is why it is so important for a daily relationship with the Lord Jesus Christ.

If a man wants to flee from his masculinity, I ask with a sincere heart that he be open, willing, and committed to discover why through sincere godly help and guidance. I encourage him to be strong and face the issue head on, allowing Satan no room to keep him locked up in secrets, isolation, despair, confusion. He must not regret the wonderful man whom God has created him to be.

5

Escaping Femininity

Denise Shick

When the opportunity came to write this book, I knew it was very important to address female GID due to the rise in calls Help 4 Families receives from friends and family who have loved ones who were born female, but strongly identify with masculine roles and characteristics. In the past, most of our calls came from family members of males who struggled with their male identity. Now, an increasing number of our calls come from people concerned about a female friend or relative who identifies as a male.

The reason for so much inquiry and confusion is due to the challenge of traditional values and recent efforts in society to perpetrate the "born this way" theory. In May 2013, the Tippecanoe School for the Arts and Humanities in Milwaukee sent home notes to inform parents of "Gender Bender Day." (Sanchick, M.)

The specific purpose of this day was to influence boys to dress up as girls and influence girls to dress up like boys. However, these experiments target vulnerable young people and can actually be injuring to their mental health. In the case of a young girls to dress as a boy can begin to feed her imagination and possibly the negative feelings or confusion that she may already have about her own gender.

Many factors come into play with this ever-changing view of femininity. The freedom and ability to be physically altered from female-to-male (f-to-m) is difficult for most people to even comprehend. But not only are such dramatic attempts being made, it's becoming fairly common—much like a new trend or fad. But neither surgery nor hormones can change the simple fact that a person born with female DNA will always be, genetically, a woman.

Society's Changing Views of Gender

By the age of two a child's perceived view of his or her gender begins to be established. If the child is a girl, she probably has already experienced being affirmed as such. Or her femininity might have been rejected-emotionally, physically, or verbally. Children remember and soak in what their culture and the people in their lives tell them.

Bisexuality has become a fad with girls who have an interest in someone of the same gender, yet also attracted to the opposite sex. This trend recently gained traction with Katy Perry's song entitled "I Kissed a Girl." Despite concern from parents, Katy Perry became a hero of sorts to many young girls who might have been unsure or insecure about their gender identity.

Some girls are sexually and emotionally attracted to other girls, but they feel that if they become a "man" they will not face the shame and embarrassment of being "gay". One mother shared: "My daughter is in denial of her same-sex attraction. Some friends have told her it would be more natural to love a woman if she were to exist as a man."

Similarly, Hollywood has long sought to demolish traditional gender identities and roles. The showcase star for gender confusion is Chasity Bono, who has become known as "Chaz". Chaz dramatically increased her notoriety when she performed as a contestant on the *Dancing With the Stars* TV program.

When I had first heard of Chaz being signed to be a contestant on this show I couldn't help but ponder the influence this would have on the young people who were watching, especially those who are already feeling inadequate in their born gender—already confused they could point to Chaz, smiling on the dance floor, and declaring to doubters, "See, Chaz is happy in his new identity." But not all smiles are real; many cover serious issues and scars that need to be healed.

Hollywood and the media carry a grave responsibility for encouraging females gender confused or who simply do not fit traditional gender stereotypes. Granted, not every girl conforms exactly as one might expect of her gender, but that doesn't mean that they should be encouraged to explore the possibility that they might have been born of the wrong gender.

Feminine Self-Hatred

Girls with GID literally often have a deep hatred of their bodies. A young woman named Sasha demonstrates a perfect example of this feminine self-hatred. Sasha wears a breast binder to hide her breasts. When she looks in the mirror she gains confidence from her male like appearance. Sasha is now considering a hysterectomy in order to stop her menstrual cycle that haunts her as a constant reminder that she is truly a woman. Sasha also suffers from depression and severe anxiety. She has been hospitalized for suicidal attempts over the past few years. Her hospitalization visits leave her feeling as if she is in a vicious cycle, searching for her identity and completeness.

Some girls who take the more masculine role in lesbian relationships begin to see becoming a man as the next logical step in their relationships. Often we hear of lesbians taking on a "dyke" appearance. Gail states, "That was me." She became involved as the masculine partner in a lesbian relationship. She then distanced herself further from looking feminine and dressed to resemble a man. Gail could not seem to become "butch" (male) enough. Before long she decided that in order to fit the role she was now playing, she needed a more masculine name. Since her name already began with G, she thought the name Gavin would be a good fit. Gail started to modify her identity to match her fantasy by starting testosterone treatments that would allow her to grow body and facial hair. She also had chest reconstruction surgery consisted of a double-mastectomy and construction of a male-like chest. She no longer identified as a woman but felt that she was no different from a born male.

Gail is an example of girls who utterly reject their femininity. They're distressed over having breasts and over experiencing menstruation. Some gender-confused girls stand up while going to the bathroom to imitate men. These girls tend to feel and believe that they would be more complete by gaining a penis and by having their breasts removed. They see their breasts as unwanted, constant reminders that they were born "wrong." Sadly some women with GID have healthy body parts surgically removed due to conflicted emotion.

Growing Prevalence of Female-to-Male Transsexuals

Female-to-male (f-to-m) transsexuals are less common than male-to-female (m-to-f) transsexuals. A report on estimated ratios of f-to-m lists 1 natal female for every 2 to 3 males (Weitze & Osburg 1996). However one must realize that with the societal shift—and with this becoming a new fad—the rate of f-to-m phenomenon may indeed rise.

Manufactured Male

The f-to-m transsexual treatment consists of testosterone treatment and a bilateral mastectomy, and in some cases a surgical creation of a pseudo-penis and testes. The manufactured penis will not work however like that of a real man. It will always need the assistance of a manual pump for obtaining erections. The f-to-m transsexual through manufactured gender and hormones will be able to attain facial hair and the body muscle like that of a male, creating a masculine body figure and a deepened voice.

Though treatments, sex-reassignment surgery, and hormones are readily available for f-to-m transsexuals, nothing can change their DNA from its natural state. Female-to-males will sometimes seek a hysterectomy in order to end menstruation. Some choose not to have sex-reassignment surgery due to the high costs involved and the possible complications that accompany such surgeries. Others choose to travel to Thailand, where they can have sex-reassignment for a much lower cost—but perhaps at greater risk.

I will never forget these words from Molly, a mother of a daughter who is transitioning: "It's just like someone who has anorexia; they look in the mirror and see themselves as something that is not reality." As Molly continued to share her heartache, she asked why mental health professionals treat anorexia, but encourage and assist someone with Gender Identity Disorder to give in to their illusion?

Possible Causes of Female Gender Identity Disorder

The typical girl desires to be feminine, like her mother. She has a natural caring and nurturing desire. But, clearly, some girls go astray. Many ask, "Why would a girl want to be a boy?" One's mind can become a battlefield, especially when the person becomes obsessed with an idea. When a female behaves as a boy, her own peers might begin to reject her, which can further damage her self-image.

If the child is encouraged to reject her femininity she will look for the needed affirmation in another role. An example of this is when a girl's parents tell her they had wished for a boy, or that life would have been easier if she had been born a boy. The girl might perceive such comments as rejection and might begin to believe that if she were a boy, her parents might love her more. She believes that her gender determines her value.

Rejection by a parent figure can be another possible source of such a desire to change genders. Sexual abuse can be another trigger. The victim may come to believe that the "male world" dominates females, and she never wants to be dominated again. She reasons that by becoming a male she can escape domination—and hurt—at the hands of men. The girl could have been sexually abused by another female, and her body could have responded to the touching, allowing her to feel that she must be gay since her body responded. The intimacy with another female could have provided an outlet for her to mesh emotionally.

Rachelle's daughter, Theresa, has GID. Rachelle said her daughter often witnessed her very own father abuse Rachelle physically, verbally, and emotionally. Theresa idolized her father.

She seemed almost obsessed with trying to gain her stepfather's love and affection. Her daughter had felt rejected by her own father and sought her stepfather's love and approval. Such domestic dynamics can cause some girls to struggle with feeling abandoned by their fathers.

Rachelle remembers her daughter preferring to play with boys and trying to imitate them. Theresa wanted to play the role of being a brother while playing house. Rachelle remembers her daughter preferring to do boy things while trying to be like them. Rachelle says, "While playing house with my friends' children, she seemed to idolize the little boy named Jimmy." Rachelle had placed make-up on Theresa for her dance recital. Her father told her "Only whores wear lipstick." Rachelle realized her daughter sought desperately to please her father. At the age of 15 Theresa had made her father very angry. Her father's anger had become violent and physical.

Theresa called the police out of great concern. He packed and left before the police arrived. Theresa loved her father and felt abandoned by someone she deeply loved. She became a cutter and by young adulthood she began to struggle with alcohol issues. She ran away from home and became involved in boy gangs. Theresa

has had several relationships with other woman and struggles with

depression and attempted suicide several times.

Another example of a daughter struggling with rejection is the

situation in which a pregnant woman resented being pregnant and,

because of her resentment, told the baby while in her womb that

she hated her. This unborn baby grew up into a young woman who

felt unloved and rejected by her mother. As a result, she attached

herself to the masculine world. She feels that her father's world is

a safer place. The relationship between the mother and daughter

have remained strained, as the mother has poured her life into her

work, leaving her daughter to feel abandoned much of her life.

Stressors that trigger gender-confusion episodes might also

include eating disorders, cutting, bullying by peers, PTSD,

borderline personality, depression, deep grief over a loss, or other

addictive behaviors. Some people mentally block out traumatic

events from their lives. There is no single causal factor. Whether it

is a control issue or a desire for escape, the root causes must be

addressed in order for the person to attain peace and healing.

In order to help understand some of the environments or causes that may attribute to a person struggling with his or her born gender, we have cited and will continue to cite anecdotal cases in this book. There are times when the issues that contribute to gender-identity issues go unnoticed until later. When one finally sees those contributing factors, it is like the proverbial light bulb switching on, and the person says, "I get it!" However, there are times when the contributing factors remain unknown for various reasons. This is a very difficult place for the struggler and for family and friends. It is vital for the struggler to want to discover why he or she feels the way he or she docs.

Addressing the Core Issues

I felt discouraged for a friend who was being treated for some psychological issues. The psychiatrist failed to dig into what brought her the point of suicide. Instead, after a brief discussion, he prescribed medications. I was well aware of her long-term emotional turmoil, and I marveled that the doctor failed to address the deeper issues that brought her to a depressed state. No one wants to deal with pain and emotional baggage, but a problem can't be cured if it remains in the dark. Healing happens in the light. It may take years to undo the damage and rejection. It is important that each layer of pain is peeled off delicately, and the patient handled with care. The value of the process and the end result is priceless.

Attunement and attachment are important tools for parents to use in preventing GID (Phelan, 2011). Secure attachment offers a stable development, brings a greater self-esteem, and initiates social competence. If GID does occur, research shows that brains of the people who report greater attachment and attunement have a better chance of overcoming pathologies (Phelan, 2011).

In our world of technology and busy schedules we seem to have little time for deep relationships. Yet *attunement* is an important tool in building a relationship with a children. Attunement gets lost when parents are absent and children are left unattended. When two people gaze into each other's eyes, they connect and communicate care, love, and affirmation. It sounds simple, but it happens too infrequently these days.

Resonation is very important as well. Resonation occurs when one person smiles and the other person smiles back, allowing each to feel the bond concurrently. Resonation provides greater self-esteem, ego-resistance, and greater social competency. Research shows that people with GID can better regulate their lives and have a chance to overcome their pathology if they know how to resonate with other human beings in authentic ways. Because of the brain's plasticity (the brain's unique ability to constantly change, grow, and re-map itself over the course of a lifetime), there is hope for those with GID. In a culture that has largely abandoned the concept of absolutes—whether in matters of morality or in matters as basic as concepts of reality—getting to the root causes of issues such as GID can be difficult. How does one get through to a person whose standard reply is, "Well, that may be your reality, but it isn't mine?"

Pandora's Box Has Been Opened

Our culture has opened a Pandora's Box and are now facing the consequences of our silence and of allowing or encouraging people to live fantasy lives rather than face the truth. Facing the truth about a loved one who has chosen to try to live contrary to his or her God-given gender is not easy, but it is necessary. Most of us can hardly imagine wanting to have healthy body parts removed, or wanting unnecessary appendages pumped in or sewn on. We can't come to grips with the desire to switch not only one's identity but also one's gender. So ignoring the issue, snickering because it's someone else's problem, or at least keeping it at a safe distance, seems to be the easiest course—until the person making that choice is a close friend or relative.

When that happens, laughing at Klinger on *MASH* or at Dustin Hoffman as *Tootsie* is no longer so easy. When the issue becomes personal, we have to ask some hard questions and pursue some painful answers. Facing up to the prospect of your son wanting to become your daughter is altogether different from reading about Tracy Lagondino (a woman) becoming Thomas Beatie (a "man") and then becoming the first so called "man" to give birth.

Decades ago, a few at society's fringes peaked and poked around "Pandora's Box," and then cracked it open. In short order, our "progressive" entertainment industry made a bundle of money promoting the pixies' escape from the box, first onto our film and TV screens, and then into our living rooms and bedrooms. Now many of our sons want to become those pixies and many of our daughters want to become burly lumberjacks, and many within the medical field are happy to buy new BMWs with the profits from the expensive body alterations required to help these confused young people "embrace their true identity."

We live in a "climate where people see nothing wrong with surgeons destroying reproductive organs and creating artificial organs for those who want them" (Fitzgibbons, Sutton, & O'Leary, 2009, p. 98).

Hormones and manufacturing a person's gender does not 'fixed' them. The inner wounds still exist. There is a negative influence in our culture to accept gender non-conformity. Sometimes we need to look deeper into a movement and its reasoning. The truth is, women like Theresa whose affected by GID deserve the opportunity to be counseled by someone who does not have personal motive, but rather one that is client motivated.

Sometimes we need to look deeper into a movement and it's reasoning. The truth is, GID is a very complex issue. The people who are impacted by GID deserve the very best help. Satan has created a way to steal not only women's identities, but daughters from mothers and fathers, sisters from their siblings, aunts from nieces and nephews. He is the thief who comes to steal a person's

true identity.

6

Sex Surgery Regrets

Denise Shick

One afternoon, while I was running some errands, I received a call from a twenty-four-year-old I'll call Nolan, who said he was seeking help for "a friend." Within seconds I realized that this call was not for a friend, but rather about Nolan. The young man said his friend had thought SRS (Sex Reassignment Surgery) would solve his gender issues. As he continued sharing his heart's desire to help his friend, he sobbed uncontrollably, asking, "Will God forgive my friend?" The despair in Nolan's voice was devastating.

I assured him that God forgives, as the east is from the west. He will remove the sins of those who ask in true faith. Yet sometimes the most diffiuclt thing to do is to forgive ourselves.

Our culture encourages and promotes views and lifestyles that lead to measures as drastic as SRS, but then refuses to acknowledge that many who go to such extremes later regret those choices. Instead, those who express such regret are often told to "accept who they really are." Below are examples of people who have regretted their attempts to change their gender.

Rob's Regret

Rob underwent SRS when he in his thirties. Now, in his sixties, Rob often speaks of regretting his decision. He feels that life has passed him by while he has been imprisioned in a body that daily reminds him of his imprudent choice. He speaks of a heart that yearns to have a wife, and of being able to have a truly intimate physical relationship with her. He tearfully laments, "If only I could go back." Though missing his male parts, Rob now dresses as a man, and has taken back the name his parents gave him at birth.

Unfortuantley, Rob's chioices cost him some family relationships. Slowly, he is restoring some of those relationships. Yet he regrets the time that he lost with those loved ones.

Katie's Brother

Katie's brother is a m-to-f transsexual. Her heart breaks as she shares of the lonelilness her brother has felt in his self-imposed life of isolations as a confused "woman". She said he rarely steps outside his house, and when she visits him, he is very depressed.

Brad or Ria?

Ria Cooper is an eighteen-year-old in Britian who has had hormone injections as part of the proccss of becoming a girl. Ria appears to have natural breats, and she wears beautiful feminine outfits. But now, after spending a lot of time and money on the treatments and wardrobe-and after two suicide attempts-Ria has changed her mind. He (see the confusion this causes) wants to be the boy, Brad he was born. Now, the question naturally arises as to whether she was too young to have been allowed to make such a dramatic, life-altering decision.

Ria says, "The hormones have made me feel up and down. One minute I feel moody and the next minutes I feel really happy.

A couple of months ago I'd had enough and took a lot of paracetamol. Just before that, I'd tried to slash my wrists and ended up in a hospital. I get these dark moods when nothing seems right."[1]

How many more Rias are out there, people who, as children, diagnosed themselves with GID? What will their lives be like in ten or twenty years? Will they have the same regrets Ria has had? Will they have gone beyond hormone treatments and had costly, expensive, dramatic, and irreversible sex-irreversible sex-reassignment surgeries? It is wrong to conclude that surgery can cure a psychiatric disturbance; it just does not make senese.

Nancy's/Nathan's Grief

Most children will outgrow Gender Dysphoira when they reach puberty. Children who have a persistent case of GID are usually diagnosed with severe gender dysphoria in their childhood.

We see this in the life of Nathan Verhelst, fourty-four, of Belgium, who was "rejected by his parents as a girl. Her transformation as a man began in 2009 with hormone therapy, followed by a mastectomy and finally an operation to construct a penis" (Damien, Oct 1, 2013 n.p). Nathan said that in the hours before her "death" (to her old identity as Nancy) she "was ready to celebrate my new birth. But when I looked into the mirror, I was disgusted with myself" (Damien, Oct 1, 2013 n.p.).

Nancy chose to end it all. Sadly, Belgium allows its citizens to choose euthanasia based on their feelings of "unbearable phychological suffering."

Not surprisingly, Nancy/Nathan felt no love from her/his mother, who commented, "When I first saw Nancy, my dream was shattered. She was so ugly," she told Belgium's *Het Laatste Nieuws.* "I had a ghost birth," Nancy's mother said. "her death does not bother me." Imagine how any child would feel when raised by such a callous mother.

Selective Recognition

What will the lives of other Rita's be like in ten or twenty years? Will they have the same regrets a Ria has? Will they have gone beyond hormone treatments and had costly, dramatic and irreverisble sex-surgeries?

The mainstream media-ignores these sad tales of regret because they contradict the popularly accepted narrative of the satisfied seeker, finally being freed from the entangling bonds of a mistaken birth.

If SRS is, as our culture now popularly proclaims, a good solution for those who are gender confused, why are there higher risk for mortalities, suicidial behavior, and psychiatric morbidies than those of the general populations? One study says, "Findings suggest that sex reassignment, although alleviating gender dysphoria, may not suffice as treatment for transsexualism, and should inspire improved psychiatric and somatic care after sex reassignment for this patient group."[1]

I remember when my father asked my grandfather to take his guns because he feared he would commit suicide. My first reaction was, "Why does no one seem to notice how distraught and ill he is?" Culture has tried to convince those who are distressed and fractured by gender confusion that SRS is their best choice. If so, then why is the suicide rate so high for those who have undergone SRS?

Chris Hyde, director of Arif, said, "There is a huge uncertainity over whether changing someone's sex is a good or a bad thing. While no doubt great care is taken to ensure that appropriate patients undergo gender reassignment, there is still a large number of people who have the surgery but remain traumatized-often to the point of committing suicde."[1]

The truth of the matter is that many transsexuals have come to regret their SRS.

7

Family Complications

Denise Shick

Families are devastated when they are hit with the news that a loved one desires to become the opposite of his or her born gender. Too often family relationships are strained and shattered through the difficulties that arise. The individual usually makes demands that are often very challenging for the family members to abide by. The families incur situations that many do not understand unless they have walked the same path. Usually the families suffer a tremendous blow to their emotional, spiritual and physical well-being.

Sophia, for example, is a stay-at-home wife and mother who has a deep need to protect herself emotionally. In order for her to prevent her husband from wearing her clothing and using her make-up, she keeps only one spare outfit in her living space. That's a coping method. She stated, "I have one outfit on while the other is in the washer." She is concerned about the psychological impact her husband's cross-dressing will have on her four young children. That's a concern needing the Lord's intervention.

I know of nothing more painful than having a loved one ask his or her family members to bury any memories of that person's true birth identity. Nothing can prepare family members to cope with hearing a loved one say that he or she wants to live and appear as the opposite of his or her birth gender. When that happens, the whole family dynamic often changes and family goes into a tailspin, grasping for their next breath.

The loved one with GID typically asks the family members to put their own thoughts, faith, and feelings aside in order to support him or her in being "true to myself." I have seen many families torn apart when various members choose sides, some conceding and others resisting. The family members who do not accept the newly chosen identity mourn a "false death" as they feel a deep loss over the one they had known. The parents and other family members have to learn how to cope with what feels like losing a loved one to physical death.

When family members support their loved one behavior and actions, they actually are enabling their loved one to do something which does not serve his or her genuine well being. Jack requested that his mom be present at the hospital during his sex reassignment surgery. His mom agreed to be there. She felt comfort in knowing she would be at the hospital if anything went wrong. She privately hoped that he would change his mind before surgery.

Needless to say, Jack did not change his mind. He felt that his mom was showing some level of support since she agreed to be present. His mother on the other was not prepared to visit her son afterwards. She admits she had a need to "mother him." She regrets this decision, years later.

Harry wanted to transition from male to female. One evening he asked his sister to refer to him as Anna. She refused at first, but after months of Harry's persistent requests, she finally gave in. One lie led to another as she had to introduce Harry (Anna) as her sister or girlfriend. When she tried to set some boundaries, Harry threatened to end their relationship.

Family members may be devastated as they witness their loved one ingesting hormones, and as they listen to their loved one's desires and plans to have sex-reassignment surgery. Sometimes family members are asked to support the loved one's gender-change endeavor by being present at the hospital the day of the surgery. I know of parents who have gone to the hospital, not to show support for the gender change, but rather out of concern for the loved one's safety. Sometimes doing so backfires because the loved one perceives their presence as acceptance of the surgery. Other times parents are openly shocked when they see their loved one missing body parts he or she had at birth.

Desperately searching for answers, one day my grandfather found himself rummaging through the attic, looking at old photos of his son as he was growing up. Finally, however, he admitted to being worn down by his son's relentless insistence that he was "born this way." My grandfather wrote the following note to my father:

> *There is nothing I can recall that would lead me to believe you were having trouble with your sex. As you grew up it was as if you had two separate people inside of you. I gave you the special name nickname 'Buddy,' as I was so certain you would grow up to be my buddy and we would enjoy life together.*

He added that he had often bailed his son out financially, which enabled his son's irresponsibility. He shared with his son that he was "tired of this vicious cycle. You are always blaming someone else when things don't go your way. It is time you start taking care of yourself."

Similarly, the father of a gender-confused daughter faces many challenges of his own. Norman's memories of his beautiful baby girl have turned into anguish as he blames himself for his daughter's emotional pain due to infrequent contact with her after divorcing her mother.

Another father grieves as he stares into the mirror while shaving. He pictures his daughter, pumped full of male hormones, standing in her bathroom, looking into the mirror as she shaves her increasingly masculine-appearing face. Each testosterone injection adds to the process of slowly stealing his daughter from him. When a father first holds his baby girl in his hands, he can't even imagine that one day he might look at her and see a face full of whiskers!

Because our culture accepts and even promotes these formerly forbidden – and not too long ago, technologically impossible behaviors, - those who are seen as stubbornly clinging to outmoded values often are pressured by their more "progressive" family members to accept "Robert as Rebecca" or "Elizabeth as Ethan." Some family members have succumbed to calling their confused child or sibling by their newly adopted name. Some who have done so later regretted it when the confused family member then felt accepted in the new role.

One mother shared that as she called her son by his new name, he began to believe that she was accepting him as her daughter. She had to explain to her son that she could not embrace him as her daughter. I have heard many times of fathers with GID want their young children to call them "mom" when they are out and about. In some instances children have been called nieces and nephews, as we see below in a note my father wrote to my mother. My mother became "sister in-law" to my father:

To Whom It May Concern:

I Becky Schmidt on 03/26/91 request my Beneficiary at the time of my death, as the follows. To my sister in-law Ruth Schmidt, also the following, nieces and nephews, Denise Shick, Clyde Schmidt, Michael Schmidt, Casey Schmidt, Anne Brown, divided as follows. Ruth Schmidt executive, that she would die before me, Denise Shick to be executive to my estate, amounts as follows. Funeral expenses and debit to be taken care of first. Ruth Schmidt, is to be paid the balance, divided equally among the nieces and nephews, that Ruth Schmidt would pass away, all of the balance to be divided among the nieces and nephews.

Signed,

Becky Schmidt

Wives can lose their own identity as they put so much effort into "fixing" their husbands. These wives become lost as they face the uncertainty of their marriage relationship with their husbands.

They lose the desire to look attractive and feminine. Often, mothers and daughters are impacted in the same manner. Many times the women in the family, as they're putting on their lipstick, find themselves wondering: *"Is this the shade he would wear?"* Or, perhaps, while putting on a bra, she recalls her husband or father's desire to have breasts. As the wife or daughter sees the mirror's reflection of her body, she might be reminded that her husband or father desires the very same "parts" she was born with. In my experience it is not uncommon for a wife to feel she is in a lesbian relationship with her husband as he increasingly tries to look and act like a woman.

In these situations the wife might want to make the marriage work, but at the point when her husband determines that he is going to transition, their marriage covenant is broken. Typically, however, the husband tries many methods to convince his wife to stay with him. But by then, usually the husband has tried manipulation at so many levels that the wife is emotionally and mentally drained. Some wives have confessed to me "I no longer have any desire to live."

I believe that at this point a part of these women's souls has died and withered away. The light of life is barely flickering in these wives. Suicidal thoughts may start to gain momentum in environments in which the husband becomes an emotional predator, devouring the wife's will to live.

In such a situation a wife may lose her value as a woman and hit bottom emotionally. Yet the message from our culture is that the wife is wrong to oppose her husband's behavior—his "fulfillment." After all, some say, these men are only "being true to themselves." Let me turn that thought around: Is it wrong for these wives to be true to themselves? How dare the culture tell these wives how they should feel? These women need a support system for their emotional survival.

I am sharing below a letter that my father wrote my dear mother as he wanted to come home after being gone for a long time.

> *Dear Ruth,*
> *Please read this letter very carefully. I have been thinking about the things that would still take place, in order for us to be able to live together. I need your response to these things, for we need to do this in order to know how you feel about it and not go into it blind.*
>
> *1st How will the neighbors react to the family?*

2nd How long will you allow me to shave my body?

3rd How often can I wear women nightgowns?

4th Do I pack my clothing and see if things will work out?

These things might not seem important, but I believe for your sake and the kids, you have to deal with these and maybe more, I am trying to be honest about the whole thing. This is very important to reply as soon as you can.

With all my love,

Harold

In multiple letters a husband shared great details of his actions to his wife. The introductions were always the same as he writes, "The kids need to read my letters to you. It might help their life in many ways." Help who? Perhaps his letters brought some "freedom" to himself, but at what cost to the children?

Recently, a wife contacted me, sharing that her children were getting horribly confused as their father sometimes dressed as a woman in their presence. The three young children asked, "Why does daddy look like a mommy, and why does he say, 'Daddy used to be a man."

A Christian Community Response

These families need comfort, support, and love, and shouldn't we, the people of the church, act as Christ would? We call church leaders to come out of their comfort zone and demonstrate a Christ-like compassion for these families. These struggling families need church leaders who will comfort, offer godly council, offer prayer support and love them through these difficult journeys. Church leaders need to learn the truth about GID. By seeking to be "Jesus with skin," they can demonstrate Christ's love for those caught in this trap and for their family members. I wrote the book *When Hope Seems Lost* to offer a ministering tool to assist ministers and church leaders (See the "Resource" section on p. 98).

In some ways, some churches have become deaf to the plea and moved on to "acceptance," leaving many souls searching. I challenge church leaders and attendees to search their hearts and ask themselves a very difficult question. Who do you desire to serve? The choice is simple, it is either God or the culture.

Doug struggles with cross-dressing. He is also considering going fully into the transsexual world. Recently he shared with me "I feel as though I'm having to walk this path all on my own. I'm still trying to find a safe place in the church where I can share my struggle. I don't understand the church. I believe we would have fewer people falling away if we had the churches support and desire to help people like me. I want to know what makes it so hard for all those who struggle with sexual sin to come to the leaders and overseers of the flocks to discuss these issues." Those are the words of someone desperately seeking a Christ-like church, not a culture-accepting church.

The cries are real. The tears being shed by lost and hurting people are real. Their inner being searches for a church that will be willing to meet them where they are, and to love them back to their God-created gender and His original purpose for them in that gender. I realize this topic is not one that most are comfortable with. I have been in churches where the elders demonstrated their discomfort over my presentation of this topic. In other cases, the congregation members were uncomfortable when they realized the focus of the Help 4 Families ministry.

The enemy of our souls doesn't cease his temptations at certain city intersections. The devil is an equal-opportunity tempter. Doug's brokenness—and mine as well—might look very different from the brokenness seen in others, but the fact is we all need Christ. The importance of reaching the churches is the reason I wrote my second book, *When Hope Seems Lost*. If you are a church leader and feel unprepared to minister to a Doug or to family members, please get this book to help you to become equipped (See the "Resource" section on p. 98).

Recently, I was interviewed on a Christian radio program. The host asked, "How can we preach the truth when we know that people will leave the church?" I replied, "We have to keep speaking the truth in love so the people know the truth. If someone is offended, then go to them afterward and lovingly show them from scripture why you said what you did." If we deny or run away from God's truth, then why would we continue with church? We must remember that God did not run away from the people, the people ran away from God.

One person's gender confusion can cause multiple issues for their family members. They can't see what's coming their way, or what's behind them. They try to grab hold of the situation only to find that it's like grabbing a fist full of fog. Families often, then, retreat into memories of better times. Affected family members often feel as if they are in a desert, spiritually starved and parched. They have a longing for God's living water and hunger for His love and embrace. Only He can meet such needs. Reliance on God must take the place of self-reliance. The family member must learn to hang on to God like none other. Facing the situation with Him gives them strength to face each tomorrow. He takes the burden to lighten their load. He pursues them to bring emotional and spiritual healing to the inner most parts of their heart and soul.

God asks you to rely on Him alone. He wants you to know that you are valuable to Him. He will pursue you and carry you through. He waits for your response to His question: "Will you let Me handle this?"

8

Steps Toward Healing

Denise Shick

Some, but certainly not all, dysfunctional families have troublesome roots, such as: alcoholism, neglect, sexual abuse, divorce, physical abuse, drug addiction, workaholic parents, physically or emotionally absent fathers or mothers, incest, verbal abuse, emotional abuse, sexual disorders, a domineering fathers/passive mothers, and/or a domineering mothers/passive fathers.

Those struggling with gender confusion learn survival skills that too often are little more than a defense developed to protect themselves from the chaos and painful occurrences they endured in their childhood homes. Unfortunately, these defenses can follow one into adult life and add to his or her struggles, especially in relationships. Even men and women of God sometimes continue to carry old wounds and painful memories. Although they have attempted to convince themselves and everyone around them that they are just fine, it is only a façade.

What's in your closet?

Make time to take stock of what is in your emotional "closet." Examine the contents of your rejections, hurts, and past wrongs, exposing what is covered behind your actions. Unexpressed emotions and buried memories can cause you to build walls, which can become a self-imposed prison. You'll then need to find the key to be released—a key that requires you to stop covering up your emotions and refusing to face the truth.

Inside your emotional closet might be fear of facing the truth; inability to deal with anger; a need to admit to heart issues such as resentment, fear, rejection, and approval seeking. Perhaps you have issues of low self-esteem, guilt from wounds that were caused by others, loneliness, and/or inability to deal with emotional or co-dependency issues. You can place those items back in your closet and close the door, failing to address them. Or you can choose to stop allowing them to be your stumbling blocks by working on them, and working toward restoring your heart and mind. Here's Paul's advice: "Do not conform to the pattern of this world, but be transformed by the renewing of your mind. Then you will be able to test and approve what God's will is—his good, pleasing and perfect will" (Romans 12:2, NIV).

It's important to understand that Satan knows your weaknesses. He wants to take advantage of you by tempting you with your own desires. Satan wants to use your desires to cause obsessions and destruction in your life. You need to detect the danger signs so that you can move forward in your healing process. Satan wants to take advantage of you, so it's best not to be ignorant of his strongholds and snares.

Remember that Satan will send enticement, entrapment, and bait your way. Honesty will help you to recognize your weaknesses so that yout able to make a stronger and wiser choices. You can't stop temptation from coming into your life, but you can stop them from becoming sinful actions. You have power over your choices. Understand that every choice follows a process, and every process has consequences.

Choices can be difficult and painful, but not even the driest soul is out of the reach of God's restoring touch. God is the rescuer when we ask Him to be and when we leave room for Him to work. Everyone has a past, but remember everyone also has a future. That future is either with God, or without Him. He knows that you have tried to pray away your transgender thoughts. But before you blame Him for your confusion, remember "For God is not a God of disorder but of peace" (1 Corinthians 14:33, NIV). He did not send the strongholds that have held you captive. Many wrongly assume that when they have prayed repeatedly for deliverance and see no answer that they must have been "born this way," and they give up and give in.

Our culture does not accept or acknowledge that a person with gender confusion might have spiritual, emotional, or psychological wounds that need attention. God wants to give you more than superficial healing. He wants to give you a deep, cleansing healing. God would not be a God of love if He allowed people to be healed only superficially. He knows that each of us needs a deep inner cleaning. God is the perfect surgeon and will use His surgical tools to cut directly into the infected wound. He will use his tools of love, truth, and grace to remove the lies and deception that the enemy had planted within. God's scalpel carefully scrapes away lies that have been accepted and exchanged for the truth.

Embracing the truth

The surgical tools of truth are very effective, but at times they also can be painful because they require that the patient abandon denial. When that happens, truth begins to shine through the areas that darkness once claimed. You begin to accept that God did not make you this way. You begin to see and understand that it was your own faulty belief system and foggy perception of who you are that had tricked you into believing you were born "in the wrong body."

Through your weakness, you reacted and gave in to the emotional needs and fleshly desires. However, by recognizing the truth, you have learned that giving in to fleshly desires satisfies only for a time, and then leaves you empty. Sometimes the most difficult task you have as is to admit to the frailty of your own heart and soul.

So, how will you move forward in the new truth you have come to accept? First, you need to be realistic about the time your healing will require. The problem took many years to develop; the restoration will likewise take a lengthy healing and restorative process. More importantly, remember that this process will require hard work. You will need to be seriously committed to the process and the time this restoration will require. God can transform our minds to His ways, when we allow Him to and cooperate with His grace (for help).

The truth means admitting that you may not have understood the stronghold cross-dressing and acting out can have in a person's life. When you started you probably thought you'd be able to control your desires, only to learn later that the desires had taken control of you. Satan seeks to devour and destroy (1 Peter 5:8) God's perfect design for His Creation—and that includes you! Few understand the power of an addiction until they find themselves ensnared in one. If you have become trapped in an addiction, quit hiding and pretending. Let us reclaim our real selves, the one God created. Claiming your born gender is one example of leaving the bondage behind as you move forward. It's a matter of choosing truth over deception.

Dealing with deep hurts

If you were molested, understand and accept, down in your heart, that you did not invite the unwanted molestation. It isn't your fault. You did not deserve to be taken advantage of. Sometimes being taken advantage of in such a way can cause a person to make choices that can damage the internal gender "compass." Satan will then use these events and choices to chain you to a destructive bondage. But if you are willing to take the time and effort, God will give you the strength to face the truth and allow healing to take place in your life.

We don't normally have the opportunity to choose our parents, children, and siblings. When an emotional need is unmet, some people search to fill that need with superficial substitutes. Though the need is met on the surface, the deep emotional wounds are unhealed. It's like placing a bandage on a severe laceration. The bandage only covers the surface while the wound festers. Some try to fix those unmet needs through other people, but only God can truly heal them. When God is invited in to heal the most painful wounds, expect a work to be done within your heart and spirit.

Perhaps you were mistreated by a parent or loved one and you vowed to be as different as possible from that person. Perhaps you believed all people of that person's gender were like that person. Maybe you're jealous of a friend who had only the best role models. Whatever the reason, remember that the wrong kind of personal vows can have a lifelong stronghold that can be very difficult to break.

Your Professional help

Pride and self-righteousness will only keep you from getting the help you need. There are times when a professional therapist might be able to assist in dealing with some of these wounds.

Shame and guilt are two of Satan's best tools. Don't allow these tools to stop you from receiving good medical or psychiatric care as needed. Proverbs 16:18-19 warns, " pride goes before destruction, a haughty spirit before a fall. Better to be lowly in spirit and among the oppressed than to share plunder with the proud" (NIV).

Accountability

Having accountability partners will be very beneficial for your ongoing care. A person who gives a regular account of his actions to an accountability partner is much less likely to give in to his desires than one who sees himself as unaccountable. After a long time of being vulnerable and accountable to an accountability partner, eventually the person might reach a point when he can resist without his partner. It's important to remember that, whether we like or not, "… each of us will give account of himself to God" (Romans 14:12, NIV). We might escape accountability here on earth, but we will not bypass being held accountable to God in his kingdom. Allow godly men and women to come alongside you and help you in this area.

Changing people, places, and faulty beliefs

You may need to avoid the places and people who remind you of the past or cause you to fall in your spiritual and emotional healing. Satan will set you up for a time to try and test you. It's simply what he does best. Prepare your heart and mind to resist being tempted to hang out with, or call on transgender "friends". You have been tricked into believing that you are "transgender." In the first book of the Bible we read that "God created mankind in his own image, in the image of God he created them; male and female he created them" (Genesis 1:27, NIV). God did not create a third gender or a genderless person. So do away with labeling yourself "transgender," "gay," or "bisexual" and discover who you are in Christ, in whom all things were created. (Colossians 1:16).

Stop believing past accusations that have been spoken to or about you. A false belief system can lead to spiritual atrophy and spiritual death. On the other hand, God's word says, "'For I know the plans I have for you,' declares the LORD, 'plans to prosper you and not to harm you, plans to give you hope and a future" (Jeremiah 29:11, NIV). If you transitioned or are currently living out of God's plan, does He still have plans for you? You bet! Come unto Him and allow Him to show you the plans He has for your life from this day forward.

Your Pastoral Support

Ongoing pastoral support is important for your spiritual well-being and growth. For far too long the enemy has camped out in your heart and soul. He has worked steadily to trick and deceive you to return to the darkness which he once held you captive.

God's word brings life to the soul: "As the deer pants for streams of water, so my soul pants for you, my God " (Psalms 42:1, NIV). Give your soul what it requires to replenish what has been stolen from you.

Allow God to help you refocus on the destiny He has for you, one step at a time. Remember to stand guard over what you are feeding your mind and spirit. You have the right to take back the ground Satan has stolen from you.

9

What Do You Really Want

"Kerry"

My mother instilled two things deep into my heart when I was young. The first was a great and abiding love and respect for my parents and God. The second was her profound disappointment that I had not been born a little girl. I know she deeply loved me. But she had no idea how her casual comments concerning my gender took root in my heart. Nor could she understand how other factors would eventually reinforce those innocent comments and create a perfect storm of circumstances that began a long struggle in my soul.

I have always been a solitary person. When I was three or four years old, my mother often found me sitting under the sink, in the dish pan, with the cupboard doors shut. I felt safe there in the dark, and I could sit there for hours just thinking and listening to the sounds outside the doors. I guess, looking back, I've been hiding like that most of my life, a spectator to life but not much of a participant.

As far back as I can remember, I believed I was a failure and that no one could love the *real* me. After the birth of my older brother, my mother said she hoped that she could have a little girl. Instead, she got me. My father, on the other hand, had always wanted a son who was athletic, as he had been when he went to school. But I was no athlete; my interest was in music; I wanted to become a musician, like my mother and my brother.

Although my parents loved me, I always felt that I was a surprise, since I was born ten years after my brother. To make matters worse, I seemed to excel at nothing except finding ways to get into trouble (like the time I put a flat washer around an electrical plug and stuck it back in the receptacle; I got in a *lot* of trouble for that one).

One day, when I was about eight years old, I found some of my mom's clothes lying on the clothes hamper in the bathroom and decided to try them on. As I looked at myself in the mirror something seemed so right about it; for some reason I didn't feel like a failure anymore. I felt good; I felt I had purpose and worth. So, from time-to-time I snunck into the bathroom and dressed in my mother's clothes—until she caught me. When she asked me what I was doing, I told her I wasn't doing anything (which of course was ridiculous since her clothes were lying there and I was wearing her make-up). So she called my father into the room and together they tried to shame me so that I would never do that again. Unfortunately, shame had the opposite effect: I cross-dressed all the more; I just became much more careful about how and when I did it.

When I was nine my mother was diagnosed with cancer and after that sometimes was in the hospital for months at a time, and my dad spent most of his free time with her. They couldn't afford a babysitter, so I was home alone and had a lot more time to dress up and discover my "feminine" self after I came home from school. This routine went on for about three and a half years, until my mother passed away.

After that, because of all the medical bills my mother's cancer treatments had accumulated, my dad and I had to move into a less expensive house. My dad worked long hours to pay off those bills, and I rarely saw him. So, again, I had a lot of time to be in my female persona around the house. No wonder that by the time I was twelve I was absolutely sure I was a female spirit trapped in a male body.

I desperately wanted to be a girl, but that was the late sixties, and I lived in a very small town in the middle of the Bible belt, where transsexuals were something you saw only on shows like Phil Donahue. I could think of no one to talk to about the feelings that had become deeply rooted in my heart.

One day, out of desperation, I prayed with all my heart that God would change me into a girl. After all, didn't Jesus say in Matthew 17:20 that if I just had faith He would answer my prayer and that nothing would be impossible? So I prayed with all my heart that God would change me into a woman, and suddenly I started to shake; I thought I could feel my body really starting to change. So I continued to pray even harder. And even though part of me was excited about becoming female, I was scared that things seemed to be happening to me that I had no control over. I began to panic. How was I going to explain this to my family—to my friends? So I stopped my prayer and just sat there trembling, thinking about what was happening to me, and ever so slowly the feeling that my body was changing subsided.

I know this was probably all just psychosomatic, but I was still filled with fear and awe because for the first time I got a sense of how big and how powerful God really is. It was all very scary; God had gotten my attention.

Not long after that experience, my dad remarried and we went to live at my new stepmother's house. I deeply resented my stepmother and spared no opportunity to tell her so. My open resentment of her caused a lot of discord in the house, and after three years and several rebellious episodes, including my stepmother finding some of her clothes in my closet, she gave my father an ultimatum: Either I had to go, or he and I both had to leave. So my dad eventually kicked me out of the house. I lived on the street and in various places for a few months until a pastor took me in. I lived with him until I graduated from high school and found a job.

Soon after graduation I married a girl I'd been dating, hoping that marriage would make a man out of me and take away my cross-gender desires. But, before long I was actually cross-dressing in front of my wife and using money we desperately needed to survive to purchase wigs and feminine clothing for myself. During this dark time in our lives I was utterly absorbed in my pursuit of becoming a woman. Eventually my wife told me that she could not take it any longer. If I didn't get help, she would take the children and leave.

So, I sought out the pastor who had taken me in and explained my situation and asked for his help. He in turn set up an appointment with a psychologist, who eventually diagnosed me with gender identity disorder. The psychologist told me that I would not find a resolution to my problems until I had, as he put it, "Conformed my outside to match how I saw myself on the inside." His solution was to enter counseling to dissolve my marriage. Meanwhile, I would begin my gender transition by taking female hormones, begin dressing full time in woman's clothing and go through counseling with him until I received the necessary letters for surgical reassignment surgery. Then, I could *legally* become a "woman".

I went to that appointment to see how I could save my marriage. Instead, I was told that the best thing I could do was to dissolve it. But, despite the psychologist's expert opinion, somehow I knew that was not the right answer. No matter how appealing the thought of finally becoming a woman seemed at the time, in the end I knew it was just wrong.

So, I began to seek out other local pastors and Christian counselors, thinking they might have the answers to my cross-gender feelings, but despite all the prayers and the searching, in the end I could find no answers. The only verse I could find in the Bible about cross-dressing was Deuteronomy 22:5: "A woman must not wear men's clothing, and a man must not wear woman's clothing. The LORD detests people who do this." This verse only served to reinforce my feelings of failure and inferiority; it seemed that not even God could love me.

What was wrong with me? All I wanted was to be "normal," whatever that was—or at least integrated, not a woman stuck in a man's body. I could not find help, or a way to overcome my desire to be a woman, so my wife finally had enough; she divorced me and moved out of state with our children. The pain in my heart from all these events was so deep it was hard to even breathe. Only the thought of being separated from God and stuck in hell forever kept me from committing suicide.

One day, after I got home from work, the pain of it all was just too much and I began to weep bitterly. I cried out to God from the depths of my pain; it seemed that things couldn't get any worse, so I begged God to forgive me. Much to my surprise, I could feel Jesus' arms wrap around me. I felt a warmth and a love that I'd never felt before.

The authenticity of that moment changed my heart forever. I still didn't understand why all this was happening to me, but I knew for the first time that God really did love and care about me. Perhaps, there was an answer for me after all. So, I started to really seek after God, I began to study my Bible and became involved in a small group at the church I was attending. Even though I was seeking God, I still sometimes found myself going back to cross-dressing. It was a crutch when things got really tough, but afterward I was always filled with intense shame and guilt.

The feelings that had brought me so much inner peace and pleasure in the past became a "hook in my flesh" that I could not seem to overcome. The more I prayed and tried to ignore my feelings, the more powerful they became. They were always on my mind, in my conscious thoughts and in my dreams, and I could find no peace until I gave into them. So I would pray and try to ignore my feelings, and so the cycle went, again and again and again.

After a few years I fell in love and married a woman I had met at my work place. I knew that God had brought her into my life, so I told her about my cross-dressing before we got married. I'm sure she thought that it was a problem that I had already dealt with — and to be honest I was afraid to tell her otherwise. But it was still very much a part of my life, and I found myself privately cross dressing with her clothes.

One day, when I put her things back in the drawer, I did not put them back as she had arranged them and she questioned me about it. Just like the situation when my mother caught me, I knew

I was stuck. So instead of lying, I admitted what I'd done and promised not to do it again. But it was a promise doomed to failure. I couldn't stop myself, and I knew it. A few weeks later I woke up early and went outside and sat on our porch swing and begged God to kill me because I could not bear to live that way any longer. Something had to give; either I would finally find deliverance from these feelings, or I would be forced to fully succumb to them. But, I could not live between two worlds any longer.

In answer to prayer, a couple weeks later I found a website called *Parakaleo*. *Parakaleo* is a Greek word that means *to gently exhort*, and that is what Keith Tiller, the author who wrote *Parakaleo,* did for me. He began to show me that my gender confusion was really just a symptom of a much deeper problem. I discovered that I was not really a female spirit inside a male body; I was a man trapped in the sins of idolatry, envy, and lust. While the Bible had little to say about cross-dressing, it had volumes to say about these sins. I wanted to be something I could never be and experience things that were not mine to know. I wanted to be a pseudo-woman, but that was a facade hiding my deep-seated feelings of failure as a man.

King David wrote in Psalms 139:13-16, "You made all the delicate inner parts of my body and knit me together in my mother's womb. Thank you for making me so complex! Your workmanship is marvelous—and how well I know it. You watched me as I was being formed in utter seclusion, as I was woven together in the dark of the womb. You saw me before I was born. Every day of my life was recorded in your book. Every moment was laid out before a single day had passed."

To say that there had been some kind of "cosmic" mistake, or a birth defect caused by an incorrect hormone wash in my brain and that I was really a female living inside a male body was to call God a liar. My acting out on my cross-gender feelings was a declaration that somehow I knew better than God, my Creator, who and what I was. My life and relationship with God had, up to that point, been based on my "feelings," not on the truth of God's Word.

I had to face the fact that I was not a mistake, I was just a lost, hurt soul—a sinner like everybody else. I had built my life on lies and perceived truths, rather than on the bedrock of God's Word (Matthew 7:24-27). As I began to contemplate these things in my heart I could feel the chains that had bound my heart begin to break, and even though there was still a lot of junk down in my heart, I knew that I was at last on the road to freedom and sanity from this prolonged nightmare.

One day, months later, as I was studying the Bible I could sense the Lord asking me, "My son, what do you really want?" After I thought about it for a while, I replied, "Lord, I want to learn what it is to overcome, I want to finally be done with this cycle of sin in my life, and I want to live in the freedom, holiness, and power You promised me in the Scriptures. But most of all, Lord, *I really want to know You!*" Then the Holy Spirit reminded me of Matthew 16:24, 25: "Then Jesus said to His disciples, 'If any of you wants to be my follower, you must put aside your selfish ambition, shoulder your cross, and follow me. If you try to keep your life for yourself, you will lose it. But if you give up your life for me, you will find true life.'"

Then, the Lord said to my spirit,

You fail because you are fighting this fight in your own strength, and you end up surrendering to your fleshly desires instead of surrendering your fleshly desires to Me. If you would only have faith and trust in Me, you would find that the battle has already been won for you at the Cross. However, to claim this victory, this grace, you must die to these desires, pick up your cross and follow Me. Do you want to be My disciple? Will you let Me fully into your heart? Will you let Me heal and deliver you? My son, what do you really want?

The following verses were poignant:

Galatians 5:24 (NLT): *Those who belong to Christ Jesus have nailed the passions and desires of their sinful nature to the cross and crucified them there.*

Romans 6:3-7 (NLT): *Have you forgotten that when you became Christians and were baptized to become one with Christ Jesus, we died with Him? For we died and were buried with Christ by baptism. And just as Christ has been raised from the dead by the glorious power of the Father, now we have new lives. Since we have been united with Him in His death, we also will be raised as He was. Our old selves were crucified with Christ so that sin might lose its power in our lives. We are no longer slaves to sin. For when we died with Christ we were set free from the power of sin.*

Colossians 3:5, 6 (NLT): *So put to death the sinful, earthly things lurking within you. Have nothing to do with sexual sin, impurity, lust, and shameful desires. Don't be greedy for the good things of this life, for that is idolatry. God's terrible anger will come upon those who do such things.*

People ask me how I walked out of gender confusion. The

simple truth is that I finally surrendered all my pain, passion, hopes, and dreams to Jesus. I learned that we are all survivors, and we try to cope with the pain in our hearts the best we can. We sometimes try to mask the pain with drugs, alcohol, or even retreating into a fantasy world. But as Proverbs 14:12 declares, "…there is a path that seems right, but in the end it leads to death". A person can be sincere in his or her beliefs, but if those beliefs are based on feelings and not on God's Word, then regardless of sincerity, they are still ultimately wrong.

It is hard to give up the things we know and are comfortable with, but for me it was much worse to base my life upon a lie or an illusion. I've heard it said that "hurt people hurt people." I hurt a lot of people that I claimed to love and care about, while selfishly chasing after something I could never really have. I had come to believe I could be happy only if I could live out my fantasy as a woman, but I discovered that my fantasy was nothing more than a mask to escape my sense of failure and pain.

Galatians 2:19 says, "When I tried to keep the law, I realized I could never earn God's approval. So I died to the law so that I might live for God. I have been crucified with Christ. I myself no longer live, but Christ lives in me. So I live my life in this earthly body by trusting in the Son of God, who loved me and gave himself for me."

Now that I am walking on a road less traveled (Matthew 17:13, 14), I have come to realize how fortunate and blessed I am to have a wife, friends, and especially a Savior who didn't give up on me, who helped me get through some very tough times.

No man is an island unto himself, and no man can make it all alone. What I lacked as a young man (someone to share my burdens with) I now thankfully have. By God's grace I am becoming the integrated human being the Lord designed me to be. The Lord has even begun to restore my children and grandchildren to me, and I have made peace with my first wife, who has also been restored to the Lord.

All in all, even though I have a long way to go, things are now working out pretty well for me. The more of myself I give to Jesus, the more of Jesus I have in myself. The more I deny myself and give my life away for Christ's sake, the richer my life becomes in the fullness of my Savior and Lord, Jesus. I could not be happier being anyone other than the man God created me to be.

10

A Journey Of Healing

"Linda"

From my earliest memory I wanted to be a boy instead of a girl. Somehow I just knew that if I had male genitalia, my life would be complete. I prayed repeatedly for God to make me into a boy and became obsessed with my pursuit. For instance, when playing with one of the neighborhood boys, I regularly asked him to drop his pants and "show me the goods," so to speak. He readily complied, and I stared in fascination at the male genitalia, jealously longing for what I didn't have. Whenever playing "house" with friends, I always chose the male role and would stuff my pants to simulate my dream of having male genitalia. It was all I could think about as a child.

In the fourth grade, I learned about sex-reassignment surgeries and vowed I would have the operation as soon as I was old enough and had the money. About the same time, I was exposed to pornography, which developed into sexual addictions that would span the next twenty-two years. During much of my childhood, I spent hours alone in my room feeding my sexual fantasies, always envisioning myself as the male counterpart rather than the female. I was especially mesmerized by urinals and frequently took "sneak peek" trips into men's public restrooms and pretended I was using a urinal. No one else noticed because I looked so much like a boy, which made my day. The very sight of a urinal became arousing and eventually developed into a sexual fetish as an adult.

In junior high, when all the other girls were interested in makeup and boys, I found myself attracted to women—especially older teachers who were strong yet nurturing. I desperately wanted to be held and comforted by a woman, which then developed into sexual fantasies. I was horrified by my attractions, but I dared not tell anyone.

Around seventh grade, I started to consider the logistical difficulties of having sex-reassignment surgery. Where would I get the money? How would I tell my family? You can't just be Linda one day and David the next. I considered running away as soon as I was old enough to have the surgery without ever telling my family. But I loved my family, and I knew that would devastate them. Even though I wasn't a Christian at the time, I started to have a sense that sex-reassignment would not be God's will for me. I made a conscious decision at that point to try and conform to society's expectation of me to look more like a girl in order to fit in. But, inside, I still longed deeply to be a man, and the attractions to women became increasingly difficult to resist.

When my body began menstruation, I could have sworn my life was over. I envied the boys around me whose voices were beginning to change, and I mourned the fact that mine would never change like that. Instead, I had to submit to wearing training bras and being inconvenienced by monthly periods. Being female was a curse, not a blessing, I thought.

I got saved during my junior year in high school, but within days, I began doubting my salvation experience because my struggles didn't go away, as I thought they would. Yet I knew God had done something in my heart, and I wanted to follow Him. I got involved with my church youth group and, for the first time in my life, felt that I had friends who loved me. But the closer I got to Christian females, the more I struggled with my attractions and sexual addictions. I was miserable but couldn't tell anyone. I tried growing my hair out and even dating guys—thinking that being physical with a boy would "cure" me—but it just made me want to be male all the more. I tried to conform and even wore dresses on special occasions, but inside it always felt like I was wearing a costume, like dressing in drag.

In college, I got involved with a campus ministry and developed a deeper relationship with God, praying and reading my Bible regularly, even sharing Christ with the lost. I eventually became a student leader, despite the fact that I was deeply attracted to every woman who mentored me and was enslaved to sexual addictions behind closed doors. I prayed privately for God to please take my transgender desires away, hoping no one would ever know.

My senior year in college, I attended a campus ministry conference elective on overcoming habitual sin. The speaker quoted James 5:16, "Confess your sins one to another and pray for each other so that you may be healed," stressing how important it is to get your sin into the light in order to be free. I was deeply convicted and knew I had to confess my secret to my campus pastor if I was ever to experience freedom.

It took all the courage in the world to finally tell my campus pastor my lifelong secret. In fact, I seriously considered suicide as a way out, but I knew that would devastate my family. When I finally confided in my campus pastor, I expected him to react with shock, horror, or condemnation, because I was a leader in the ministry living a double life. But instead, he responded to me in love, assuring me that he was committed to finding me the help I needed. I couldn't believe it. I walked away from that conversation with a fresh revelation of God's grace. I had always felt God hated me and condemned me for my sin. My campus pastor's reaction was a living illustration of the Father's heart toward me. For the first time, I discovered that being completely transparent with another person was very healing. That day in 1994 was my first step in what would be an eleven-year journey toward freedom.

My campus pastor met with me a few times and eventually connected me with a professional counselor. The next decade was full of ups and downs as I sought healing. I read every book I could find on homosexuality, listened to tapes, attended conferences, and met with multiple counselors from ex-gay ministries as well as general Christian counseling. It was a slow process, as there were not a multitude of resources at that time to help women struggling with transgender issues. In fact, well-meaning Christian counselors told me they had seen homosexuals and lesbians set free but never anyone transgender, so I should do my best to cope this side of heaven and know that I will be totally free when I die. Despite their discouragement, the Lord gave me supernatural assurance that He would completely heal me and that the transgender issues would be a thing of the past. Nevertheless, I thirsted deeply for maternal nurture. I seemed to get worse before I got better, falling into sexual immorality with another woman from my church. I eventually repented and broke off that relationship, realizing my fantasy of being a man who slept with women would never fill the deep void in my soul. By God's grace, I resolved to tug at the hem of His garment and not let go until I experienced the freedom Jesus died to give me.

As I continued to pursue healing, the Lord gave me a spiritual mother who was only a few years older than I but spiritually much more mature. I was deeply attracted to her, yet she wasn't phased by my struggles and began to invest in me relationally in a wholesome way. I found myself wanting to be just like her (much like a daughter might want to emulate her mother), so she helped me buy more feminine clothes and gave me advice concerning makeup and mannerisms. My outward appearance began to change, but inwardly, I still believed the lie that it was better to be a man, and I was still battling attractions to women.

In the fall of 2005, the Lord eventually led me to meet with an inner healing prayer counselor. Over the course of a week, we spent hours praying through a lifetime of deep emotional wounds, mostly related to my family. I forgave those who hurt me, let go of bitterness, renounced inner vows, and repented for my wrong responses toward those who had wounded me. I embraced the

Cross, and we closed every door I had opened to give the enemy legal ground to influence my life.

One of the most profound wounds had to do with my mother wanting to give my dad a son (whom she hoped to name David). Though my mom never verbalized her desire for me to be a boy—I always felt genuinely loved and cherished by my parents just as I was—my spirit picked up rejection even from the womb. Despite being born full-term, I weighed only three pounds, fourteen ounces because part of the placenta had died. It was as if my mom's body was trying to abort me, and I was literally being starved in the womb. Due to my low birth weight, I was immediately whisked away to an examining room instead of lovingly coddled in my mother's arms. After I was born, I spent my first few days in the hospital isolated in an incubator, and the doctors kept me at the hospital for observation for sixteen days. When my parents finally brought me home, my mom chose not to breastfeed so that Dad could be included in the bottle feedings. Thus, any chance of maternal bonding was lost. The disconnect with my mom was exacerbated by our distinctly different personalities and other family dynamics that persuaded me to reject my own gender. It was the perfect storm.

As my counselor and I prayed about my experience in the womb, Jesus spoke to my heart: "You don't have to try to fit their mold [to be a boy]; you've already been molded perfectly into who and what I want you to be…. They may have wanted a boy, but I have veto power…. It's not better to be a man than a woman; nor is it better to be a woman than a man. It's best to be exactly who I created you to be."

That week, the Lord spoke to my heart similar healing words, which dispelled all the lies I had believed. I cried and cried as the Lord spoke graciously to me, and for the first time in my life, I saw a tender, compassionate side to the Father that I wasn't aware existed. It was as if I could literally feel His hands holding my heart. My lifelong yearning to be held and comforted by a woman was met in the tender arms of my heavenly Father.

After that powerful encounter with God, I had a newfound contentment in being a woman and was set free from my sexual fetish/addictions, which were essentially a counterfeit to the comfort I could find only in my Father's arms. As I continued to walk out my healing, I eventually started experiencing genuine attractions toward men. It was as if I was going through delayed puberty at age thirty-four, which was both awkward and thrilling to finally experience the mystery of sexuality according to God's design. God had transformed me from the inside out and accomplished the impossible. I still feel like I'm living a dream.

Though I wanted to share my testimony immediately after everything happened in 2005, the Lord had me wait. I see His sovereignty in that now, as I needed time for my healing to be tested and to prepare me for the warfare that lay ahead. I stayed silent for eight years until the Lord gave me the green light to go public upon my eighth-year anniversary of freedom, a "new beginning" of sorts. Now, as a forty-year-old woman, I am finally coming out of the closet in a redemptive way, sharing my story with others to bring hope and restoration. I'm grateful for all the pastors, counselors, faithful friends, and especially my supportive parents who walked with me during the healing process. The eleven-year journey towards freedom was totally worth it. The length of the journey itself has given me empathy for those who are currently struggling to break free from similar issues and sometimes feel hopeless. Healing from sexual brokenness is rarely instantaneous—it's more like peeling back layers of an onion one at a time—but if we will hold fast to the truth of God's Word and determine never to give up, we will experience the freedom that Jesus died to give us. God promised: such *were* some of you (1 Corinthians 6:9-11).

11

Cross-Dressing and Christianity

Anonymous

In or about October of 1996 I experienced an onslaught of temptation and spiritual warfare in the area of cross-dressing. This strong wave of desire to dress in women's clothes was totally out of the blue, although it was something that I had experienced before in my life. At times, the temptation was so strong that it was all I could think about. As a result, I could not focus on the normal activities of life. Fortunately, I found help and hope. Today, after over thirty years of dealing with this, I can truly say, "Thank God I'm free!"

I was an only child, so the closest thing to siblings I had to play with were my girl cousins who were close to my age. Of course, playing with girls meant playing girls' games, like playing house and dress up. The overall effect was that I was raised in a feminized environment where the female role was dominant and the male role was passive. In my inner being, I found the feminine role attractive, but modeled after the passive male image.

One of my earliest memories was when I was about five or six and my mother had me try on clothes she was sewing and hemming for my female cousins. As I grew older and into adolescence, I had a strong desire to try on girls' clothes. I remember finding discarded dresses, wigs, earrings, etc. and trying them on and feeling an erotic excitement. I formed a strong association at that time between wearing feminine clothing and sexual release. Later, in times of stress, I retreated to that same activity to feel relief. This was my secret world where I could fantasize about being beautiful and soft.

On the outside, in many other ways I was a typical boy. I was active in Boy Scouts, worked on cars, liked to go target shooting, and was not feminine at all—just "a nice guy."

Marriage Years

In college, I met and married a wonderful girl to whom I am still married. In the early years of our marriage, my cross-dressing desires were only occasional. I never told my wife of my urge to cross-dress because I was in a state of denial. I really didn't see cross-dressing as a bad thing, just an odd thing.

After we had been married for a few years and had two son's, the pressures of work and family seemed to increase my desire to cross-dress. I looked for any occasion to cross-dress, especially Halloween. An unexpected opportunity came at a church banquet when one of the ladies of the church asked me if I would dress up as Dolly Parton. This was a real treat because not only could I cross-dress, but I could do it right at church!

During those years, I felt guilt and confessed the cross-dressing as sin, but eventually I did it again. I never really admitted to myself I was a cross-dresser.

Even though cross-dressing was a source of release, it was also a cycle of guilt and shame. Every time I did it, I felt shame. The shame caused me to feel even worse about myself than I did before, and I was then tempted to cross-dress again to relieve that shame, and so on.

Eventually, I got to the point where I just decided to "white knuckle" it and quit cross-dressing. Whenever a temptation did come along, I just ignored it. I really didn't give a thought to cross-dressing for two or three years. I managed to totally repress any feelings or thoughts about cross-dressing. Then the Lord engineered what I believe to be an incredible set of circumstances.

The Spiritual Warfare

We were happy in our church at the time, but on the day of our nineteenth wedding anniversary, the Lord impressed both my wife and me that we should move on. "But to where?" we wondered. We decided to visit a new church much closer to home, and we were so led by the Lord that we joined. One of the first sermon series was titled "Everyday Victory for Everyday People." This study in spiritual warfare would prove to be life changing.

After going through the study, my wife approached me one day and said that she felt a need to confess a stronghold in her life so that she might be delivered. I already knew about her stronghold, and I said, "Well, since you confessed yours, let me confess mine."

In the previous days, I had started to experience some of the old temptations of cross-dressing. I said, "You know I struggle with smoking, but I also have another problem that I have struggled with all my life." At that time I told my wife that I had strong urges to wear women's clothes. I was also quick to say that I was not asking for her acceptance of any cross-dressing. I also explained that the battle at that point was mainly in my mind and that I had never been unfaithful to her. She handled my confession very well and said she would pray with me about how to deal with this problem.

I decided that I needed more information about cross-dressing, so I logged on to the Internet and started doing searches on "cross-dressing" and "Christian." This proved to be a mistake. I learned everything the world had to say on the topic, and I learned the arguments that other Christians had constructed to justify the behavior. At this point, I became very confused and deceived. I saw so many images of guys like me transformed into beautiful women that I was really tempted to seek out a makeover for myself.

At that point the temptations and thoughts were almost constant. I was having dreams about being dressed as a beautiful woman, and those dreams set me up for the rest of the day thinking about such things. It was hard for me to work or do anything else with those thoughts constantly bombarding me. I even fantasized that my wife would go along with and accept my behavior. I was truly deceived. I was getting concerned that I might start acting out my temptations in public.

I was typical of many male-to-female cross-dressers in that I was otherwise masculine in appearance and actions. I also had absolutely no desire for relations with other males, so homosexuality was not part of my problem. It was at this point that I realized I had a clear-cut decision: either choose the ways of the world or follow after God. I loved the Lord more than I loved the urge to cross-dress, so I chose to get Christian-based help.

Coming Into the Light

As I shared this with my wife, she suggested that I get Christian counseling. Almost every resource I found said that cross-dressing could not be cured. Even many of the Christians who had testimonies on the Internet told of how they knew that it was all right to cross-dress; to them it was not a sin, but something fun to do. The only resource I could find on the Internet that dealt with cross-dressing as a sin was First Stone Ministries. I was glad to learn they were in my home city.

The first person I spoke with was Stephen. Stephen was the first person to sit down with me and show me Romans 1:18-32. Although I considered myself a mature Christian and student of the Bible, this passage took on a whole new meaning to me. For the first time in this entire episode, I saw that I had been deceived by "the lie" of the enemy. Stephen assured me that since Jesus was not a cross-dresser and our model, then we should pattern our lives after Him.

After my initial visit with Stephen, I started meeting on a monthly basis with a female counselor named Kim. Before I started meeting with her, I did not know whether it was best for me to meet with a male or female counselor. As it turns out, I feel that she was the perfect person to counsel me. I really needed the female perspective on my problem and also on my relationship with my wife.

A passage that she shared with me that really helped during times of temptation was Romans 6:21-22: "What benefit did you reap at that time from the things you are now ashamed of? Those things result in death! But now you have been set free from sin and have become slaves to God, the benefit you reap leads to holiness, and the result is eternal life."

Whenever temptation arose, I recalled this verse, and it helped me to ask, "Is this going to benefit me?" The answer was always "no." So instead of simply ignoring the temptation, I dealt with it in a rational way.

Around Christmas time, I made a special trip to my parents' house to talk with them. Although I didn't share specifics about my problem, I did ask many questions about my upbringing. I discovered some things, and I also learned that they had no memory of some events that were significant in my memory. One of the significant things that happened was hearing my parents say that they never expected me to be perfect. Whether it was true or not, I felt that they expected me to always be a good boy, never get into trouble, always make good grades, etc. As a result, something in me wanted to rebel against that expectation, but I never did rebel openly—just in my private world.

About two months after that visit with my parents, the voices in my head started to die down. One night when I was on a business trip, I had one thought too many and got angry enough with the enemy that I resolved to get rid of this thing one and for all. I knew that I was weak, but the Lord is strong. Under Jesus' authority, I gave the enemy and his demons their marching orders back to hell.

Soon I started seeing things much more clearly. I also was able to bring things out into the light with family, which really helped. The more I talked about this with my wife, the more deliverance I received.

A major resource that helped me during this initial time of coming into the light was T.D. Jakes' book *Loose That Man and Let Him Go*. I found it to be an excellent resource in helping me to learn what it means to be an authentic man of God. A foundational verse that came to mean much to me (and still does) is 1 Corinthians 13:11: "When I was a child, I talked like a child, I thought like a child, I reasoned like a child. When I became a man, I put childish ways behind me."

I realized that cross-dressing was like playing the childish game of "dress up," like I used to do with my cousins when I was a child. Cross-dressing also tends to be self-centered, with the cross-dresser expecting others to accommodate their behavior even to the detriment of their families. I could either stay in a childish condition or I could move on and be a man. I chose to be the man God wanted me to be.

Learning to be a man patterned after God's plan was a matter of learning the truth and modeling after Jesus. I realized that a lifetime of being raised and taught by women had unknowingly feminized me. Actually, I think many men today share this condition. I don't mean to be sexist, because certainly both male and female models are needed for a balanced upbringing. The problem is that males and females approach life from different perspectives, and, being exposed to largely the female perspective, I developed gender confusion.

At this point, my wife ministered to me in two very tangible ways. First, she affirmed my manhood verbally. This was powerful, especially when having sex. Secondly, she helped me upgrade my wardrobe. I think one of the reasons I was drawn to cross-dressing was because I felt women get to wear more stylish clothes. One of the things we did was to buy me some new suits. We got a great deal on some high-quality suits at a local discount clothing store, and they really helped me feel better about myself.

Something else I started doing at that time was "reality checks." A practical example of this was when I reasoned through the issue of my self-esteem. I had always seen myself as unattractive, and I think this also contributed to the cross-dressing urges. While in my confused state, I liked the thought of being beautiful. So, I decided to do a reality check at Wal-Mart one day. While walking through the store I started counting how many people, both men and women, were truly attractive. I still had two unused fingers after the count!

Admittedly, Wal-Mart is not where the "beautiful" people hang out, but still I realized that by far most people are average at best and some are just downright ugly. I don't intend to be mean about this, but the reality is that physical beauty is a fleeting fantasy for most people. I also had to come to terms that dressing up in women's clothing didn't make me a ravishing beauty either!

For the next few months, the cross-dressing temptations and urges died down tremendously. Only once in a great while did I think of cross-dressing. When a temptation would come my way, instead of simply dismissing it or ignoring it, I dealt with it. For example, I would examine the thought and say in my mind, "Lord, I know I am the man you made me to be. I know you love me just the way I am. In the name of the Lord Jesus Christ I command Satan and his demons to flee." This worked without fail.

Then, one Saturday morning I awoke feeling free for the first time in many, many years. I know it sounds odd, but it was like an overnight final transition happened. Not only were there no cross-dressing temptations or feelings, but also the appetite for other fleshly actions were gone. I felt clean and free. The only thing I can figure is that God healed me while I slept.

Is cross-dressing a sin?

This is a common question, because if cross-dressing is not a sin, then it shouldn't be a problem. You will find differing opinions on this, many of which are constructed by Christians (and non-Christians) who wish to justify cross-dressing as a harmless activity. I don't want to condemn anyone as "sinner," because I have many other sins myself. I also understand your urges. So please look at these as things to consider, not as a condemnation.

It is true that within the Bible the only direct reference you will find on cross-dressing is in Deuteronomy, buried in the Judaic code. If we use that verse for a reference we are on shaky ground, because most of us do things like eat pork, which is also in there. Besides, the blood of Jesus has set us free from the law to follow a higher law of grace.

In my early struggles I reasoned that cross-dressing was not a sin because obviously men wear and have worn wigs for many years, actors wear makeup, etc. Although each piece of the picture can be taken alone as harmless human activity, when you combine all of the pieces for the overall effect of trying to pass as or become a person of the opposite sex, you have transcended into an entirely different realm. If cross-dressing was simply wearing a dress but acting like a male, then one could perhaps make the point they were doing a bad imitation of Milton Berle. But if you follow the path of many male-to-female cross-dressers you will find it leads to learning how to walk, talk, and act like a female.

By shedding your masculinity and over-developing the feminine, you are stepping outside of the role God has for you. This concept is even more important if you are a husband and father. It is very clear in Scripture that God has ordained a specific order for the family, where the husband is the spiritual leader. I know from experience that you can't be the masculine spiritual leader of a family while also cross-dressing. One reason for this is that the spiritual leader should be active and not passive. Transcending into the female role or image is usually a passive role.

Another problem when male children are involved and the father models a passive image. The children are likely to carry that image into their own marriages and experience all kinds of difficulties. Personally, it was very difficult for me to even discuss this subject with my two sons, much less let them see me in the act. My sons and I have a great relationship, and I am teaching them the importance of active leadership in the home. Please don't misunderstand me; I'm not advocating a domineering, heavy-handed approach. I'm talking about leading our families as our loving, heavenly Father leads us.

Also keep in mind that something can be a sin even if there is no direct reference to it in the Word. You must submit an issue to the "whole test" of the Word. In other words, is the practice consistent with the overall teaching of the Bible? It is entirely possible to construct all kinds of arguments to justify a particular sin, even in the presence of numerous New Testament references indicating otherwise. One current example of this is the justification of homosexuality as being scripturally permitted.

The Bible also speaks to the issue that some things are permissible, but not all things are expedient, or wise. So, we can reason that some common-sense and judgment is needed to make the call. If cross-dressing is a problem in your relationship to God, your wife, or anyone else close to you, then you might consider it as one of the not-so-expedient things to do. I consider myself to be the kind of believer who can "eat meat sacrificed to idols" and it does not bother me in the least. In other words, I am not a legalist. I don't like to live by rules alone, but some are needed to establish boundaries.

While searching for an answer to the question of cross-dressing being a sin, I realized that I was looking for a black-and-white literal answer in the Word, but a black-and-white literal answer was not there. My reasoning was that if the prohibition was not there, it was okay to cross-dress. Later, I realized that was the same attitude the Pharisees had in Jesus' day. They strained at observing all of the "must do's," but they created all kinds of ways to follow the law literally while breaking it in spirit. It occurred to me that on this issue, I had become a legalist!

Let's define sin as missing God's perfect mark. As Christians we know that "all have sinned and come short of the glory of God" (Romans 3:23). We also know that "the wages of sin is death" (Romans 6:23). The good news is that Jesus forgives all our sins when we turn to him for forgiveness with a repentant heart.

I believe cross-dressing is a sin because:

It is deception. Yes, most of us to some degree modify our appearance to cover imperfections and to look our best—although sometimes the modifications look worse than the imperfection! However, to equate this with being completely transformed to look like the opposite sex is a huge leap.

It violates God's ordained gender role for a person. God doesn't make mistakes, but Satan can take small hurts and flaws in our upbringing to cause gender confusion. This gender confusion can cause many kinds of relationship problems. A cross-dressing father is a confusing model for children. Cross-dressing is normally a very self-centered activity. It is not healthy for marriage relationships.

The real test of whether or not something is a sin is your comfort level in doing it in front of people you go to church with. For example, would you feel at ease dressing up and attending church "en femme"? If the answer to this question is "no," or if you feel guilt over cross-dressing, then it fails this test.

I do know that for many men who are in conflict between cross-dressing and their faith, the compulsion to cross-dress is a spiritual bondage. You dream about it at night, you read about it, you fantasize about it, and before long you want to go public. I spent many hours on the Internet looking at websites of other cross-dressers. When anything goes to this point of compulsion, there is a spiritual stronghold. The Lord is to be the center of our attention and the object of our praise. When I was set free from the bondage, I could finally see the issues much more clearly. It also helps to have someone to speak openly with. The more you bring the issue into the light the less power the bondage has over you. It is a very freeing experience to "confess your faults one to another that you may be healed" (James 5:16).

Finally, ask the Holy Spirit to reveal this answer to your own spirit. I can only give you my perspective. You must be convicted in your own spirit as to the right and wrong of cross-dressing before you can change.

Is it possible to change?

Most secular psychologists will tell you that a cross-dresser might go into remission, but will relapse during times of stress. They also say the same about homosexuality. I can't give you my long-term story yet, but I know I'm free from any desire to cross-dress. I can also point you to others who have, for many years, been set free from cross-dressing, homosexuality, and other areas of sexual brokenness. Of course, the secular media usually doesn't report those cases.

Yes, there is hope! It's not easy and it's not quick, but you can be set free by Jesus Christ. The first step is to follow the Lord's way and not the world's way. You must repent of your sin and ask the Lord to heal you. Cross-dressing is a symptom of an inner hurt. To deal with the cross-dressing, you must first deal with your inner wounds.

In breaking the cycle of compulsion, you will also need to deal with spiritual warfare. An excellent resource for this is found in Neil Anderson's books. Those titles are found in the "Resource" section of this book.

Healing prayer, where your past and present hurts are healed by the Holy Spirit, is how the Lord ministers to you. You will likely need someone to intercede for you in this area, but it is one of the most powerful ways to be healed. Leanne Payne has written a wonderful book, *Crisis in Masculinity by Leanne, Payne*, which describes the healing prayer process.

Am I the only one?

By no means! I don't know of any firm statistics for cross-dressing people who go to church, but if cross dressing is like any other activity, then the percentage of people in the church with this addiction is only slightly less then in the secular society. If this is true, then somewhere around two percent of men in our churches cross-dress. The problem is that not many people are aware of this or even believe it.

How do I tell my wife and family?

This is something that many cross-dressers really struggle with. In my case, I know my wife so well that it was very natural to seek her help. But keep in mind that I was coming from an attitude of repentance and confession. I would advise you to get Christian counseling in sexual brokenness issues to decide when and how to tell your mate. You and your family will need support, and a Christian counselor can be the person to help you through the rough spots. You will need to trust the Lord to prepare the hearts of those nearest to you.

Why Should I Stop cross-dressing?

I struggled with this question myself. At first I felt almost a grief at giving up a fetish-like behavior I had clung to for comfort for almost thirty years. I can now say it was the best thing I ever did. My relationship with my wife and family is so much better than it was before I made the choice. I'm not proud of my past thoughts and actions of cross-dressing, but I am glad I made the choice to follow God's leading in my life.

Actually, stopping cross-dressing was a result of dealing with all of the hurts and wounds of my past, taking them to the Lord, and getting healing from Him. I simply tried quitting before, but it never lasted because I was treating the symptom and not the problem. As my wife remarked, "I had no idea there was even a problem in our marriage. Everything was just going along fine." The trouble was that I was living in my own private fantasy world and not dealing with reality. I was the spiritual leader of our family in name only.

A Final Word

Keep seeking the Lord. He will reveal all truth to you and "the truth will set you free" (John 8:32). In my victory over cross-dressing, I found it to be more of a truth battle as opposed to a power struggle with the enemy.

Look down the path to see where cross-dressing leads. If you examine closely what is on some of the more popular websites, you will find graphic descriptions of bisexuality and infidelity. What goes in our minds usually works its way out into practice. Ask yourself if this is really what you want in your life.

Many in the Christian community have grown to see adultery as the "big sin" to avoid. But, in doing so, we condone other behaviors that undermine the marriage relationship almost as much and are just as sinful.

Consider what would happen if someone found out about your cross-dressing. There is great truth to the saying "Your sin will find you out." So you need to give this some consideration before engaging in something you will later regret.

Finally, and most importantly, God loves you with an everlasting love. You were in His thoughts when He created the world. He knows your every hurt and your every need. When you come to the end of yourself and feel you can go no lower, God is there to welcome you home. He and the angels will rejoice!

The following verse describes my motive in taking a stand and motivation for making this information public:

> *Now the Spirit expressly says that in latter times some will depart from the faith, giving heed to deceiving spirits and doctrines of demons, speaking lies in hypocrisy, having their own conscience seared with a hot iron, forbidding to marry, and commanding to abstain from foods which God created to be received with thanksgiving by those who believe and know the truth. For every creature of God is good, and nothing is to be refused if it is received with thanksgiving; for it is sanctified by the word of God and*

prayer. If you minister the brethren in these things, you will be a good minister of Jesus Christ, nourished in the words of faith and of the good doctrine which you have carefully followed. But reject profane and old wives' fables and exercise yourself toward godliness (1 Timothy 4: 1-7).

12

Beauty from the Ashes

"Taynawin"

My desire to know God the Father on a deep, meaningful level and allowing room for God to heal areas in my life is where my true healing began. My story began as a small redheaded baby, not wanted by her mom or dad, placed up for adoption and taken in by her grandparents. They did the best they could and provided a strong Christian foundation, but still, because of age differences, there were some unresolved voids in my life. We parent the way we were parented, unless we break that cycle. I now seek to break the cycle.

Even at an early age I knew something was different about me—about my attraction to girls, about dressing like the boys and playing with the boys. I tried to become one of them. Despite my parents' assurances that I was not, family members often asked if I was gay. Me? Never! Yet one day my biological father told me that he would make me have a sex change if I didn't "straighten up"!

Because a male family member had sexually molested me when I was a child, my trust in males quickly became distorted. Even though it was so long ago, I remember the violation in complete detail; some memories haunt me in my dreams to this day.

I was adopted and never felt that I fit in with my family. I felt that I was an outcast, a "black sheep." I had red hair and freckles, and was often teased because of my boyish looks. I wanted to be a boy. I tried to hide the feminie aspect of my body appearances through my clothing choices. I even got boyish haircuts. Everything about me reflected a boy. It wasn't until my junior year in high school that I grew tired of the name calling and tried to become more like a girl, at least on the outside. Still, as I grew older and went on to graduate from high school, and then throughout college, my friends and family members often questioned me.

Because I'd been brought up in a Christian environment and wanted to maintain my Christian image, I created an outward feminine disguise that caused me great internal conflict. Yet, throughout my life, God provided wonderful godly women who nurtured me and pointed me in the right direction. I thank God for them to this day.

Still in my disguise, I began dating and dreaming of marriage and children. Meeting a man from God, whom I had been praying for, became my motivation for getting over this internal conflict. Much to my disappointment, meeting, falling in love, and marrying the man God gave me was not the cure.

Life, work, and becoming mother to two precious boys simply became new "garments" in my disguise. After almost seven years of marriage—years of suppressing something that needed to be dealt with—my desires erupted like a volcano. In tears, I shared with my husband this unbearable secret from my past that I could no longer hide or fight. I listed the various options for ending the marriage, but he chose none of them. Instead, he encouraged my exploration.

Later, when my feelings for women grew stronger, he began to get concerned about our marriage. My cycles of indulgences and repentance continued. That our marriage survived them is a miracle. My husband knew that God had brought us together, and He would bring us through, even though I was not yet ready for that.

Behind my husband's back, I continued to try to deal with the issue on my own, but the temptations were becoming more than I could resist. Late at night, with my family in bed, I began exploring—from chat rooms, to email meetings to, eventually, numerous affairs. My husband knew something was wrong, but our problems had grown so severe that neither of us cared any longer.

I threw myself into my work—and into this new lifestyle. I went to gay bars and parties; a whole world new opened to me. I finally *felt* free, like I belonged and was accepted for who I *thought* I really was. I thought I had found the real me. I was a mom by day and someone completely different at night; I lived for the night—as though the night would actually hide my new lifestyle.

I met several women in my search of this person I felt I'd longed to be all my life. I was convinced I'd fallen in love with one woman, and that made my once internal conflict external. I had to choose; it was her or my family. I chose her. We were together almost three years before my night life started catching up with me.

Drinking slowly became my escape from this pressure that began to consume my life—even my dreams when I tried to sleep. I began feeling there was no escape. Trying to be two different people was killing me emotionally. I had met and fallen in love with this woman I'd always secretly dreamed about, but my life was out of control.

Where could I go, who could I talk to? No one seemed to understand. But God didn't give up on me. He put in my path a friend whom I began to trust. She loved me unconditionally, yet she refused to support my lifestyle. For once in my life I was developing a healthy, close friendship with another woman. I could tell her everything and still she would always call me the next day and pray for me. But I still had to fall further.

Watching my life, and my once strong Christian values, disappear before my eyes, I slowly became a ticking bomb. My closest friends, my family, my lover, they all knew something was wrong, as I pushed them away. During this time my partner was also ready for more and wanted me to choose.

At times I wanted to kill myself rather than deal with the pressure of the choice I now faced. I could see no relief. At times I was happy; I felt as though I was on top of the world. Other times I found myself weeping before God and everyone around me. I was a basket case. I could barely get out of bed each day and put one foot in front of the other. How had I endured this double-life since childhood? I knew I was hurting my family, but why couldn't they just accept the new me? I began to question my Christianity and whether I was actually born this way. None of it made any sense to me. I was on a mission—a mission that almost destroyed my marriage, my family, and my own life. I knew that at some point either I'd kill this other me, or it would kill the me God had created.

In desperate need of help, I fell back on my face before God.

No more secrets, something had to give. I started looking over the Internet for help. I learned there were many others like me, caught in this trap and longing to escape. I began ordering books, CDs, anything on same-sex attraction. Facing this fear and learning that I was not the only one in world like this became encouraging! With my unconditional friend cheering me on with prayer and support, God was restoring my confidence in Him and in myself.

Proverbs 18:24 says, "A friend sticks closer that a brother." I now had two such friends. All these transpiring events began to bless me and open my eyes that something else was at work here in me. A friend and I drove 5 hours away for a ministry support group meeting. It was at the meeting that I learned painful steps that I needed to take to get my life and my family back.

Now with new friends, a witness beside me, my best friend, to help hold me accountable God began to move in my life! All the uncertainty and fear I had carried since childhood began to disappear. This deep dark secret was coming out yet my friends and family loved me through my pain. Next was the decision to return home to my family and my husband and walk out this healing journey. It has been a steep climb and I begin every day knowing that God created me, and I am His and He is mine. Change? YES, it is possible. I am going to leave it all to Him that created me.

I did not choose to have same sex attractions or my gender issues, but I did choose to act on my feelings and longings which opened a huge door to sin that flooded my life and family. To say they are completely gone is irrelevant, but I can honestly say I am not controlled by those feelings any longer. I am determined to drive out this giant that has lived IN MY LAND for so long.

Today, I look back and am just amazed at where I have come. Now, I see myself through the eyes of the One who created me and concentrate on my friendship with Him as He speaks to me through His word. I have learned a lot about the roots of same sex attraction and have come to terms as to why I had such strong tendencies. With this knowledge the days get easier and easier. I am glad I asked for help: "Ask and you shall receive, seek and you shall find" (Mathew 7:7). Although, sometimes I have not been in a place where I have been willing to receive the answer – it is available for me. Jesus said, "You shall know the truth and the TRUTH will set you free" (John 8:32). I long to keep my heart pointed in the right direction and to find the true me that God created me to be.

God has blessed me with so much unconditional love through this journey. He is truly faithful! Day by day He is restoring the years "that the locust have eaten" (Joel 2:25). I love my husband more than ever, daily learning to turn it ALL over to God. I am not where I want to be, but I am not where I used to be. Day by day God is bringing beauty from the ashes. [2]

Conclusion

As you have learned from reading these faith-based testimonies, freedom from gender confusion, is indeed possible. We are reminded of the words of Jesus as recorded in Matthew 19:26: "With man this is impossible, but with God *all* things are possible" (emphasis added); as for the sexually broken, Jesus promises that change is indeed possible: "…and that is what some of you *were*….but you have been [set free] in the name of Jesus…." (1Cor 6:11, emphasis added).

In the chapter, "Cross-dressing and Christianity," the author discussed how the idea of cross-dressing was his way to neutralize his feelings of inadequacy as a man. Cross-dressing had become adaptive and was his "…secret world where [he] would fantasize about being beautiful and soft." But, deep inside he knew this was not God's intent for him, and that God had made him a man who was indeed wonderfully made, and adequate just as he was. Finally, after 30 years of dealing with cross-dressing he revealed the freedom he found. The author exclaims to the reader, "Yes, there is hope! It's not easy and it's not quick, but you can be set free by Jesus Christ.... to deal with the cross-dressing, you must first deal with your inner wounds."

In the chapter, "What do you Really Want," Kerry revealed an understanding of his troubled past. Kerry's mother was disappointment that he has not been born a girl. Consequently, he would shun his own masculinity. He felt he was a failure for not being the girl his mother always wanted. Leaning to that which seemed palliative at the time, Kerry would cross-dress. Kerry revealed his journey, one that was spiritual, and one that ended in his understanding of God's grace. Kerry's healing was evident through his faith. Kerry said, "People ask me how I walked out of gender confusion. The simple truth is that I finally surrendered all my pain, passion, hopes, and dreams to Jesus."

In the chapter, "A Journey of Healing," the author discussed how she wanted to be a boy instead of a girl, and how she vowed one day she would undergo sex reassignment surgery. However, her journey took a different path and she shared, "Jesus spoke to my heart: 'You don't have to try to fit their mold [to be a boy]; you've already been molded perfectly into who and what I want you to be…. They may have wanted a boy, but I have veto power…. It's best to be exactly who I created you to be.'"

In conjunction with testimonies, this book was meant to be educational and helpful in purpose. The chapter, "Escaping Femininity" discussed some of the dynamics necessary to understand female gender confusion and on the same token, the chapter "Fleeing Masculinity" discussed, through case illustration, some dynamics necessary to understand male gender confusion.

Understanding and responding to families affected by gender confusion is also important, therefore the chapter on "Family Difficulties" assisted in this process. One person's gender confusion can cause multiple issues for all of his or her family members. Most families feel abandoned and alone. They can't see what's coming their way or what's behind them. They try to grab hold of the situation only to find that it's like grabbing a fist full of fog. Affected family members often feel as if they are in desert, spiritually starved and parched. They have a longing for God's living water and hunger for His love and embrace. What is needed is a Christian community response. Those that are hurting are seeking a Christ-like church, not a culture-accepting church.

Despite the current societal trends to give hormones to children and adults with gender identity disorders, the chapter on "Dangers of Hormone Therapy" reveal that hormonal therapies interfere with the natural biological direction of one's body and chemistry does not go without consequence. The use of these hormones can contribute to many problems and it appears hormonal interventions are simply not a safe course for individuals, and for especially children, to take.

Sex reassignment surgery, like hormonal therapy does not change the fact that one is genetically male or female. Often times those who have undergone their surgeries have regrets. The chapter "Sex Reassignment Surgery Regrets" helped to provide a greater understanding of the real life painful regrets that these surgeries bring. For example, Rob now in his sixties, speaks of regretting his decision. He feels that life has passed him by while he has been imprisoned in a body that daily reminds him of his imprudent choice. He speaks often of a heart that yearns to have a wife, and of being able to have a truly intimate physical relationship with her. He tearfully laments, "If only I could go back." Though missing his male parts, Rob now dresses as a man, and has taken back the name his parents gave him at birth. Unfortunately, Rob's choices cost him. Slowly, he is restoring broken relationships, yet he regrets the time that he lost with those loved ones.

The chapter "The Shifting of Society" discussed how science and educational systems have been ransacked with political correctness and ignores the dangers of gender confusion and the possibility of change. Never before has transgenderism been so politicalized. Despite our culture's shift, it is imperative for people of faith to resist caving in to the culture's gender messages. We are in a fight like none other before, and we need to persevere, as Paul did. Despite being imprisoned, Paul continued to reach other inmates with the truth of God's Word. Many today are trying to silence the truth that God made each of us truly male or female. There are Christian ministries that desire to follow after God's own heart, proclaiming the truth that God gives everyone a gender at birth, and it is not up to us to choose our gender. Though the battle is intense, Help 4 Families Ministry, Parakleo, Restored Hope Network (RHN), PFOX (Parents, Families & Friends of Ex-gays), and Courage International are just some of the organizations found that are persevering despite Satan's attempt to silence the truth.

.

Resources

While being mentored in ministry, my mentor assigned several book readings. We would then review them together. Though I had personal experience with these issues due to my father's struggle, I was able to gain a deeper understanding on spiritual, emotional and gender brokenness through out the reading assignments.

It is my sincere hope that the 'assigned' readings provided will be beneficial for you as well.

Books

A Wife's Perspective by Denise Shick and Help 4 Families

A Parent's Guide to Preventing Homosexuality by Joseph & Linda Nicolosi

Bold Love by Dr. Dan B. Allender & Dr. Tremper Longman III

Bondage to Bonding by Nancy Groom

Crisis In Masculinity by Leanne Payne

Dangerous Affirmations by Denise Shick and *Help 4 Families*

Desires In Conflict by Joe Dallas

Don't Call It Love by Patrick Carnes

Gender Recognition by Don Hollocks & Keith Tiller

Healing The Masculine Soul by Gordon Dolby

Healing the Shame that Binds You by John Bradshaw

Healing Your Heart of Painful Emotions by David A. Seamonds

He Can Not Be She by Gae Hall

Making Peace With Your Inner Child by Rita Bennett

My Daddy's Secret by Denise Shick

Pain And Pretending by Rich Buhler

Pure Desire by Ted Roberts

Restoring the Christian Soul by Leanne Payne

Released From Bondage by Neil Anderson

Secret Keeping by John Howard Prin

Sexual Healing by David Kyle Foster

Sexual Idolatry by Steve Gallagher

Sheep In Wolves Clothing by Valerie McIntre

The Broken Image by Leanne Payne

The Healing Presence by Leanne Payne

When Hope Seems Lost by Denise Shick & Help 4 Families

When Men Think Private Thoughts by Gordon MacDonald

Internet Resources

The intranet is full of web sites and information, yet locating truthful information on cross-dressing and transgenderism can be challenging at times to say the least. To help you out here, we have listed a few web sites that we hope will be helpful to you.

Help 4 Families (www.help4families.com) is designed to give you the encouragement, loving support, and open-handed approach towards restoration in a Christ centered environment. Many times family members and their loved one's feel isolated with their current situation. Yet Christ reminds us that He is with us, no matter what our circumstances are. Help 4 Families is a ministry that cares about where you at this moment and in the tomorrows ahead. The ministry is founded on the love and grace of our Lord Jesus Christ.

Keith Tiller of **Parakaleo** is the founder of Parakaleo (http://parakaleo.co.uk/mission). Parakaleo is a Christian referral and resource agency, based in the United Kingdom, dedicated to providing a biblical response to transgenderism, gender confusion, and related restorations of scriptural truth.

Restored Hope Network

(http://www.restoredhopenetwork.com) is a group of ministries and individuals committed to serving those seeking Christ-centered answers for sexual and relational problems.

Walt Heyer is an author and founder of **Sex Change Regrets** (www.sexchangeregret.com). Walt is a former transsexual who returned to his God-given gender after a relationship with Jesus Christ.

Another valuable resource is the **NARTH** (www.narth.com). The members of the NARTH are highly qualified professionals who understand the importance of theraputic models that are sometimes necessary for a persons healing process. NARTH offers research, books and articles that are helpful in understanding issues at a psychology point of view.

Bibliography

Ablow, K. (2011, September 2). Don't let your kids watch Chaz
 Bono on 'Dancing with the stars'. FoxNews.com. Retrieved
 from, http://www.foxnews.com/opinion/2011/09/02/dont-let-
 your-kids-watch-chaz-bono-on-dancing-with-stars/

Allen, F. (2010). DSM field trials discredit APA. Retrieved from,
 http://www.psychologytoday.com/blog/dsm5-in-
 distress/201210/dsm-5-field-trials-discredit-apa

American College of Pediatricians (n.d). Retrieved from,
 FactsAboutYouth.com

American Medical Association policies: Continued Support of
 Human Rights and Freedom, Nondiscrimination Policy, and

Civil Rights Restoration. (2011, May 16). Retrieved from,

http://www.ama-assn.org/ama/pub/about-ama/our-

people/member-groups-sections/glbt-advisory-

committee/ama-policyregarding-sexual-orientation.page?

American Psychological Association, Task Force on Gender

Identity and Gender Variance. (2009). *Report of the Task*

Force on Gender Identity and Gender Variance.

Washington, DC: Author.

American Psychiatric Association, Official Actions. (2012).

Position statement on discrimination against transgender

and gender variant individuals. Washington, DC: Author.

Andersen, T. (2013, February 17). Schools get guidelines on

transgender students: Officals say they are ready to put rules

into place. Retrieved from,

http://www.bostonglobe.com/metro/2013/02/17/transgender/F

HmjIUlSZo0LCMy02xF97M/story.html

Batty, D. (2004, July 29). "Sex changes are not effective," say

researchers. Retrieved from,

http://www.theguardian.com/society/2004/jul/30/health.menta

lhealth

Bayer, R. (1987). *Homosexuality and American psychiatry.* Princeton, NJ: Princeton University Press.

Damien, G. (2013, Oct 02). Mother of Belgian transsexual who chose to die by euthanasia after botched sex-change operation says, "Her death doesn't bother me." Retrieved from, http://www.dailymail.co.uk/news/article-2441468/Mother-Belgian-transsexual-chose-die-says-death-doesnt-bother-me.html

Delemarre-van de Waal, H.A., & Cohen-Kettenis, P.T. (2006). Clinical management of gender identity disorder in adolescents: A protocol on psychological and pediatric endocrinology aspects. *European Journal of Endocrinology, 155*(1), 131–137.

Dhejine, C., Lichtenstein, P., Boman, M., Johanasson, A., Langstrom, N., & Landen, M. (2011, Febuary 22). *Long-term follow-up of transsexual persons undergoing sex reassignment surgery: cohort study in Sweden.* Retrieved from, http://www.ncbi.nlm.nih.gov/pubmed/21364939

Chavez, K. (2004). Beyond complicity: Coherence, queer theory, and the rhetoric of the "gay Christian movement". *Text and*

Performance Quarterly, 24(3/4), 255-275.

Dobson. J. (2001). *Brining up boys*. Wheaton, IL: Tyndale

Evangelical Alliance Policy Commission (2000). *Transsexuality*. London: Whitefield House.

Futterweit W, & Deligdisch L. (1986). Histopathological effects of exogenously administered testosterone in 19 female to male transsexuals. *Journal of Clinical Endocronolgy & Metabolism, 62*(1),16-21.

Fitzgibbons. R., Sutton. P. & O'Leary. D. (2009). The psychopathology of sex reassignment surgery: Assessing its medical, psychological and ethical appropriateness. *The National Catholic Bioethics Quarterly, 9* (1), 97-125

Gesh, D. (2012). *Six ways to keep the "good" in your boy*. Eugene, OR: Harvest House.

Gooren, L. J., (1999). Hormonal sex reassignment. *International Journal of Transgenderism, 3*(3).

Gooren, L. J., Giltay, E.J., & Bunck, M. C. (2008). Long-term treatment of transsexuals with cross-sex hormones: Extensive personal experience. *Journal of Clinical Endocrinology and Metabolism, 93*(1), 19–25.

Israel, G. E., & Tarver, D. E. (1997). *Transgender care.*

Philadelphia, PA: Temple University Press.

Juarez, R., & Williams, J. T. (2013). Courts now are respecting

transgender rights; federal legislation lags, but cities and

states and the EEOC are demanding accommodations. *The*

National Law Journal, 35(46), 14.

Kane, M. D. (2013). LGBT religious activism: Predicting state

variations in the number of Metropolitan Community

Churches. *Sociological Forum, 28*(1), 135-158.

Knezevich, E. L., Viereck, L. K., & Drincic, A. T. (2012).

Medical management of adult transsexual persons.

Pharmacotherapy, 32(1),54-66.

Kuiper, A.J., & Cohen-Kettenis, P.T. (1998). Gender role reversal

among postoperative transsexuals. *International Journal of*

Trnasgenderism, 2(3). Retrieved from,

http://www.symposion. Com/ijt/ijtc0502.htm

Labott, E. (2011, December 7). Clinton, Obama promote gay

rights as human rights around the world. *CNN News.*

Retrieved from, http://www.cnn.com/2011/12/06/world/us-

world-gay-rights/

MacBride, M. (2013, September 20). Transgender teen voted

homecoming queen in Huntington Beach. *Orange County

News*. Retrieved from,

http://abclocal.go.com/kabc/story?section=news/local/orange

_county&id=9256575

McHugh, P. R. (2004, November). Surgical sex. *First Things*.

Retrieved from,

http://www.firstthings.com/article/2004/11/surgical-sex

Moser, C., & Kleinplate, P. (2006). DSM-IV-TR and the

paraphilias. *Journal of Psychology and Human Sexuality,

17*(3-4), 91-109.

National Education Association. (2006). *Strengthening the

learning environment: A school employee's guide to gay,

lesbian, bisexual, & transgender issues (2nd Ed)*.

Washington, DC: Author. Retrieved from,

http://www.nea.org/assets/docs/glbtstrengthenlearningenviro

ng2006.pdf

Parents and Friends of Ex-Gays & Gays (PFOX). (n.d.). Teach the

NEA how to write. Retrieved from, http://pfox.org/teach-nea-

write.html

Pfaffin, F., Boclting, W., Coleman, E, Ekins, R. & King, D,

Phelan, J. E. (2011). "Gender identity disorder: Understanding and responding" (pp. 114-134). In D. Shick *When Hope Seems Lost*. Maitland, FL: Xulon Press.

Phelan, J. E. (2014). *Successful outcomes of sexual orientation change efforts (SOCE)*. Charleston, SC: Practical Application Publications.

Phoenix, N. (n.d.). The progression of transgender rights in the workplace. Retrieved from, www.studymode.com/essays/The-Progression-Of-Transgender-Rights-In-1493842.html

Reisman, J. A. (2010). *Sexual sabotage: How one mad scientist unleashed a plaque of corruption and contagion on America*. Washington, DC: WND Books.

Sanchick, M. (2013, May 24). Fox6now.com. Retrieved from http://fox6now.com/2013/05/24/gender-bender-day-causes-controversy-at-tippecanoe

Sharp, D. (2014, February 1). Maine court rules in favor of transgender pupil. Retrieved from, http://www.bostonglobe.com/metro/2014/02/01/maine-court-rules-favor-transgender

pupil/SvRvYxXfdAcX4iMn0mWtBL/story.html

Shick, D. (2008). *My daddy's secret.* Maitland, FL: Xulon Press.

Shick, D. (2011). *When hope seems lost.* Maitland, FL: Xulon
  Press.

Van Kesteren P. J. M., Asscheman H., Megens J.A.J., & Gooren
  L.J.G. (1997). Mortality and morbidity in transsexual subjects
  treated with cross-sex hormones. *Clinical Endocrinology, 47,*
  337–342.

Wallien, M., & Cohen-Kettenis, P. (2008). *Psychosexual outcome
  of gender-dysphoric children.* Retrieved from,
  http://www.ncbi.nlm.nih.gov/pubmed/18981931

Weitze, C., & Osburg, S. (1996). Transsexualism in Germany:
  Empirical data on epidemiology and application of the
  German transsexuals act during its first ten years. *Archives
  of Sexual Behavior, 24*(4), 409-425.

Winter, K. (2012, October 22). "I was born a boy, became a girl,
  and now I want to be a boy again": Britain's youngest sex
  swap patient to reverse her sex change treatment. Retrieved
  from, http://www.dailymail.co.uk/femail/article-2224753/Ria-

Cooper-Britains-youngest-sex-change-patient-reverse-

treatment.html

Zucker, K. J., & Bradley, S. J. (1995). *Gender identity disorder*

and psychosexual problems in children and adolescents. New

York, NY: Guilford Press.

1Dhejine, Lichtenstein, Boman, Johanasson, Langstrom & Landen, 2011.
2HILLSONG UNITED LYRICS, "From The Inside Out."

Made in the USA
Middletown, DE
13 October 2015